GOING AGAINST THE GRAIN

POTTS' BARN

GOING AGAINST THE GRAIN

WHEAT-FREE COOKERY

by

Phyllis L. Potts

Central Point Publishing
P.O Box264
Grapeview, Washington 98546

Library of Congress Number 91-73963

ISBN 0-9630479-0-6

Potts, Phyllis L.
    Going against the grain: wheat-free cookery / Phyllis L.
Potts. — Oregon City OR : P.L. Potts,

    p. ; cm.

    SUMMARY: Wheat-free recipes, most of which are also
grain and dairy-free, with an emphasis on ease of cooking
and good taste.

    1. Wheat-free diet--Recipes. 2. Food allergy--Diet
therapy--Recipes. I. Title.
RC588.D53 P   641.5'631 20

Cover design by Bruce DeRoos
Book design by DIMI PRESS, Salem, Oregon
Page layout by DIMI PRESS, Salem, Oregon

From the treasure box...

I wish to acknowledge...

Husband, Ed, who tastes everything.
Natalie, who encouraged Mom's experimentations.
Son, Neal, who equates our family to a "treasure box."
Son, Harvey, who approves.
Dick Lutz for his guidance and expertise.
Bruce DeRoos who designed the cover.
Emily Orlando for her encouragement and editing skills.
Jan Anderson for introducing me to Emily Dickinson, cook.
Dr. John A. Green M.D. for always taking time.
Valerie McQuaid & Clackamas Community College who insisted that I learn "Word Perfect" and on whose equipment this collection was organized.
Nancy Harris for permission to quote from her book, <u>Emily Dickinson Profile of the Poet as Cook</u>.
John Hooley who jokingly named the book.
To all who said "Don't give up" and all who tasted and said, "Put it in the book!"

FOREWORD

Being an allergist and being myself allergic to wheat makes me uniquely qualified to comment on this book. In working with my own allergies, I have learned to cook with strange flours and semblances of flour, and most importantly I have learned to pretend that my concoctions taste "like the real thing." Now with this book, the need for pretending is past. Many of the baked items in this cookbook are as good as the real thing in texture and taste, and in some cases better. Now, instead of hoodwinking my children into eating alternative concoctions, I can invite their friends to share in the treats baked without wheat.

The management of food sensitivity is a difficult proposition in our food oriented society. What a joy it is to have recipes for wheat-free foods that even non-allergic people will savor. My patients and I are grateful for this book. Try some of the recipes and see what I mean!

John Green, M.D.

Contents

INTRODUCTION

I grew up in the big city, in Los Angeles - Hollywood, to be precise. My knowledge of country-related things was limited to stories in books and to famous stars like Lassie and Trigger. My 20 years of growing up in the city made me more aware of some unfulfilled needs that were always being pushed into the background, but it was not until my young family of 3 (4 if you count the boy in my husband) decided that they wanted to sample the country life that we made the move to Oregon. Here we gathered together the animal personalities that make up our 20 acre farm outside Oregon City. This is where we learned about the rewards of cooking and living a more natural life. It was shortly before this move, however, that an uninvited guest came into our lives - allergy!

Because my son and I were diagnosed as having wheat and dairy allergies, I had to change many things including my cooking. This book came about because I needed to organize the pieces of paper and magazine clippings, the cards and books which made up my recipe collection. With everything organized into an indexed binder, cooking has become more fun - so much time saved in searching for my favorite recipes. The book also comes about because my experience with wheat-free recipes had been such a poor one. My son would not eat my wheat-free creations. When_I developed or discovered my wheat allergy, I was devastated. My quality of life was crumbling. I was having to say "no" to so many good things.

In my job in the library at Clackamas Community College I set up a display, a couple of years ago, donated by instructor Jan Anderson which included recipes from one of her favorite poets - Emily Dickinson. One of the recipes was for "Rice Cakes." Wheat flour was not always available in the early days of this country. The cake turned out to be so moist and delicious, I began to see hope for creating other good baked products.

My Manhattan-based daughter, Natalie, knew that I was always looking for new ideas and thus one day sent me a bag of chickpea flour (called garbanzo bean flour in the West) that she had found in a New York health food store. So, I experimented and it was out of this combination of Dickinson and Natalie that many good tastes were born.

WHAT IS MY FOCUS?

Most of us are aware of the foods that we need to avoid in order to feel well and unfortunately we tend to focus on the negative rather than on the positive. Eating becomes a chore when the list of negative foods for us becomes a long one. It is downright depressing to be told that you have to cut out bread, hamburger rolls, hot dogs, pancakes, pies, cookies, cakes, pizza, and, indeed everything we ever enjoyed eating. And every social occasion includes eating. We are invited to teas, desserts, pot lucks, happy hours, weddings and funerals...all have wonderful things that we cannot eat.

> "Eating is not merely a material pleasure. Eating well gives a spectacular joy to life and contributes immensely to goodwill and happy companionship. It is of great importance to the morale."
>
> Elsa Schiaparelli - Shocking Life, 1954

My purpose is to present truly delicious wheat-free recipes in a manner that sparks an enthusiasm for cooking and eating without the ingredients which cause some of us problems. This book makes good eating attainable for those who are having to change their eating habits. It is easier on the cook who is trying to keep everyone happy, to eliminate the need for separate foods for family members. Everyone will enjoy these wheat and grain-free recipes!

About the recipes...

Since there is a longing for good foods and tranquil surroundings, these recipes have been chosen for their "country good" background. These are the older treasured family recipes that have been modified to accommodate those of us who cannot eat wheat and other grains. Substitutions are made for milk as well.

So many of us are working people who have so little time, it seems, for cooking. How do we cope with all this extra cooking for special diets? There are suggestions here for making the cook's job more time efficient. The emphasis is on simple recipes, although there are a couple of recipes that require more time, but they are so special and so good that one might want to consider them for very special occasions. There are recipes for mixes which can be stored or frozen, thus cutting down on preparation time. When I make a pan of cornbread, I dole out servings for everyone at the table. Then the rest is divided into lunch size servings, frozen in plastic bags or wrap and labeled, making very handy snacks to take with us when we need "fast food."

Considering equipment...

A food processor or blender is almost essential. They are so time efficient, and do a superior job of mixing and pureeing.

Baking dishes should be heavier metal or glass, never foil pans. It is recommended that oven temperatures be lowered by 25° if you are using glass.

Just because I have never been able to roll out a crust without a pastry cloth and stocking (rolling pin cover), I heartily recommend these items.

A timer that roars and stomps about the kitchen is essential!

A freezer can be an expensive investment, but one can often find an older used model if convenience and time are important enough considerations.

Not a necessity, but certainly helpful with non-wheat breads and meringue desserts, is an electric knife...something that one can find at a garage sale.

Considering ingredients...

When you are dealing with wheat-free ingredients, you need to overcome the lack of the taste of wheat to which we all have become accustomed. You can do this by emphasizing the best in your choice of accompanying ingredients.

Shortening

> In some of these older recipes, lard is recommended for giving a quality and texture not found with other shortenings. You usually use less, and the taste is worth it, but it should not be used every day.

If you can tolerate butter, it adds immeasurably to the taste, but margarine or shortening can be substituted for the butter in all of these recipes. Read the labels to assure they are dairy free.

Milk

When you substitute for milk in a breadlike recipe, you sacrifice lightness. A recipe which calls for milk, will be heavier with juice or water as a substitute, but it can be just as tasty.

Sugar

Sugar also gives structure and lightness to a breadlike recipe, so a recipe using honey may taste very good, but you will have a heavier baked product. Honey may be substituted for sugar in most recipes without any liquid adjustments. Use 1/2 the amount of sugar called for in honey, and lower the cooking temperature by 25°.

Xanthan gum

Non wheat flours do not have the gluten to keep baked goods from crumbling. Xanthan gum is found in health food stores and I use it extensively for holding baked goods together.

If Xanthan gum is not available, you may substitute powdered pectin, by substituting 1 teaspoon powdered pectin for 1 teaspoon Xanthan gum. The texture and taste will be slightly different, but still very good.

Flours

Most of the recipes in this book are grain-free with heavy emphasis on rice and chickpea (garbanzo bean) flour combinations. You will find that wheat-free baked products usually require longer and slower baking. It is suggested that you do not open the oven door during baking, and that you allow baked goods to cool gradually before handling. This is where the electric knife is helpful in keeping the bread or cake from flattening.

Most of the flours mentioned in this book can be readily purchased at health food stores and some can be found in stores which carry bulk foods, notably those in ethnic areas. I am able to purchase rice and garbanzo (chickpea) flours in downtown Portland in an older area market which caters to its ethnic population, plus Portland has an old mill which still produces all of the flours you could ever need! It is desirable to fresh-mill whole grain flours or at least make every effort to buy them fresh-milled. I've been told to keep them in the freezer, but have had good luck keeping them in the refrigerator in a cellophane or plastic bag with the air squeezed out.

If you are of a mind to do some experimenting with alternative flours, you might consult The Allergy Self Help Cookbook by Marjorie Hurt Jones, RN. It is published by Rodale. The tables on cooking and baking with alternative flours are excellent.

I would not dream of creating a cookbook of just wheat-free food. It would have to be appealing. It would have to be wonderful. I would have to look forward to the testing and retesting...to make sure it's good, mind you! It makes my day to have someone think what I am eating looks better than what they have!

So, when you are beginning to think all the "good" things are forbidden to you, that there is nothing worth eating, and every social occasion means eating the "bad" foods, take heart. Here is a passport to wonderful non-allergenic eating. Even though you will always have to field questions about why you bring your own food, you can always have something delicious whenever everyone else is going for the donut.

A few words about allergies...

No one can help you as well as a doctor whose area of expertise is food allergies. If you have food allergies or sensitivities, you need to be aware of the need for food rotation. Eating the same foods day after day can bring about sensitivities to those foods. Thus you cannot become dependent upon oat or corn flour and use it in all your baked goods, because you <u>can</u> become sensitive to those grains as well. To be on the safe side, you should try to rotate your food choices so as to not eat a grain or sensitive food more often than once every 2-4 days. This is where your freezer comes in. Keep a shelf or container labeled "oat", "corn", "rice", or "bean" flours. On day 1, one eats from shelf #1. On day 2, one eats from shelf #2 and so on. With everything packaged and labeled, you can grab a muffin and take it with you to that breakfast meeting.

FLOUR SUBSTITUTIONS

1 cup of wheat flour equals...

7/8 cup amaranth
7/8 cup bean (garbanzo bean)
7/8 cup buckwheat
7/8 cup chickpea (garbanzo)
3/4 cup corn flour
1 cup corn meal
3/4 cup millet flour
3/4 cup oat flour
5/8 cup potato flour
3/4 cup potato starch
7/8 cup rice flour
3/4 cup soy flour

The average use of baking powder is 2 1/2 tsp baking powder to each cup of wheat-free flour.

Use baking powder with sweet milk, never buttermilk.

Use baking soda with buttermilk.

See Rodales' <u>The Allergy Self-Help Cookbook</u> by Marjorie Hurt Jones, RN for a comprehensive explanation of alternative flours.

BREAD

"A loaf of bread," the Walrus said,
"is what we chiefly need."

Lewis Carroll - The Walrus
and the Carpenter from
Alice Through the Looking
Glass.

Bob's Red Mill
Milwaukie, Oregon

This mix makes so many good things and saves so much time.

BISCUIT MIX

3 1⁄2 cups rice flour   1 tbl salt
3 1⁄2 cups bean flour   2 tsp cream of tartar
5 tbl baking powder   1 tsp baking soda
4 tsp Xanthan gum   2 1⁄4 cups shortening

MIX first 7 ingredients well.

ADD shortening and mix well.

STORE in sealed container in refrigerator or on
    the shelf for no longer than a month.

May substitute   3 1⁄2 cups rice flour
                     1 3⁄4 cups potato starch
                     1 3⁄4 cups tapioca flour
                          or
                     3 1⁄2 cups rice flour
                     3 1⁄2 cups millet flour

This mix makes wonderful Impossible Pies, pan-
    cakes, waffles, dumplings, and coffee cake.

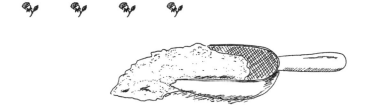

BISCUITS

3 cups Biscuit mix (p. 3)
2⁄3 - 1 cup water or milk

PREHEAT oven to 350°.

COMBINE and let stand 5 minutes.

KNEAD dough about 15 times adding flour if
     sticky.

ROLL out to 3⁄4" thickness.

CUT with floured biscuit cutter.

PLACE about 1" apart on unbuttered baking sheet.

BAKE 25 minutes at 350°.

You may also want to save time by spooning the
     dough into an 8" round cake pan, and
     baking for about 45 minutes.

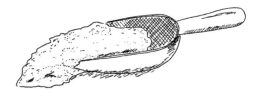

CINNAMON ROLLS

Using the above recipe...

LET dough stand 5 minutes.

KNEAD about 15 times.

ROLL out to 1⁄2 " thickness in the shape of a rect-
angle.

SPREAD with melted butter.

ADD cinnamon and brown sugar to taste and roll
up.

SLICE roll into 3⁄4" slices.

BAKE 15 minutes at 350° on a cookie sheet.

WHEN cool spread with mixture of powdered
sugar and a few drops water or orange
juice.

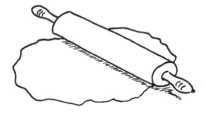

If you haven't any Biscuit mix, here's a recipe for 1 batch of...

BAKING POWDER BISCUITS

¾ cup rice flour   1 tsp salt
¾ cup bean flour   ¼ cup shortening
1 ½ tsp Xanthan gum   ¾ cup water or milk
4 tsp baking powder

KNEAD for 20 seconds, adding rice flour if sticky.

ROLL ¾ " thick.

CUT out biscuits

TRY to allow biscuits to stand for 10 minutes in a
     warm place before baking. (This is if you
     have time!)

BAKE at 425° for 25 minutes.

              or

SPOON the batter into an 8" round pan and bake
     at 350° for 40 minutes.

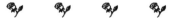

CHEESE BISCUITS

2 cups Biscuit mix (p. 3)	1/2 cup grated cheddar
2 tbl onion flakes	or parmesan cheese
2/3 cups water (or milk)	poppy seeds

COMBINE the first 3 ingredients.

SPREAD in a 9" x 11" square or 9" round pan.

SPRINKLE cheddar on top.

TOP with lots of poppy seeds.

BAKE 40 minutes in 325°.

BEER MUFFINS

2 cups Biscuit mix
2 tbl sugar
6 oz beer, room temperature

MIX all ingredients together and knead about 6
    times.

DROP by tablespoonfuls into greased muffin pans.

BAKE at 350° for 35-40 minutes.

PANCAKES

2 1/4 cups Biscuit mix (p. 3)	1 egg, beaten
1 tbl sugar (helps browning)	1 1/2 cup milk or water

MIX Biscuit mix and sugar.

ADD egg and milk or water, and mix well.

LET rest for 5-10 minutes.

COOK on hot, oiled griddle for 3-4 minutes until browned on both sides.

makes 10-12 cakes

WAFFLES

Same recipe can be poured into preheated waffle iron and baked until brown. Makes about 3 waffles.

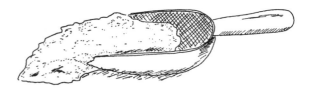

Dr. Green's recipe for pancakes makes very good bread for sandwiches. Make a big batch and freeze some. Buckwheat does have gluten in it, in case you have to avoid it.

BUCKWHEAT PANCAKES

1 cup buckwheat flour	1 tsp soda
1 cup rice flour	1 egg
2 cups soy milk or water	2-3 tsp brown sugar
optional - 1/4 cup sesame seeds	

MIX thoroughly and cook on a griddle for 2-3
    minutes each side.

Makes about 16 cakes

❀   ❀   ❀   ❀

BATTER
(for fish or...)

1 cup corn or bean flour	1 cup milk (or water)
salt & pepper	1 beaten egg

FRY coated fish in hot oil until brown.

❀   ❀   ❀   ❀

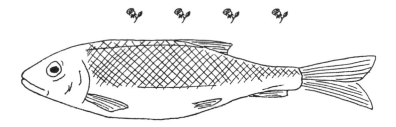

ORANGE COFFEE CAKE

2 cups Biscuit mix   3 tbl orange marmalade
3 tbl sugar   3 tbl orange juice concentrate
1⁄4 tsp nutmeg   1⁄4 cup firm butter
1 tbl grated orange peel   1⁄3 cup Biscuit mix
1 egg, slightly beaten   1⁄4 cup brown sugar
2⁄3 cup milk or water

PREHEAT oven to 400°.

GREASE and flour one 9" round pan.

COMBINE 2 cups Biscuit mix (p. 3) with sugar,
        nutmeg & peel.

BEAT egg with milk.

ADD liquid mixture into dry ingredients to dampen.

SPREAD batter in pan.

BLEND marmalade and orange juice concentrate.

SPREAD evenly on top of batter.

COVER with topping of butter, 1⁄3 cup Biscuit mix
        and brown sugar - crumbled.

BAKE in 375° oven for 40 minutes.

SERVE warm with drizzled powdered sugar icing.
    1 cup powdered sugar
    1 tbl hot water
    1⁄4 tsp vanilla

THIN with drops of water if necessary.

❧   ❧   ❧   ❧

The recipe for the perfect loaf of wheat-free bread is elusive, but the experimenting goes on... This raises beautifully!

CORNBREAD

1 cup yellow corn meal	1 tsp salt
1 cup rice flour	1⁄3 cup oil
1⁄4 cup sugar	1 egg
2 tsp Xanthan gum	2 cups milk or water
2 tbl baking powder	

STIR liquid ingredients into dry ingredients until
        just blended.

POUR into well-buttered 8" square pan.

BAKE at 350° for 40 minutes or until done.

SERVE warm. Good with creamed chicken/fish.

Optional: Add grated cheese to top before baking.

❧   ❧   ❧   ❧

A British version of an American favorite...the biscuit, these are even better the next day.

OAT SCONES

⅓ cup oil
2 tbl honey
2 tbl warm water
1 tbl lemon juice
1-2 cups oat flour
2 tbl baking powder

¼ cup rice flour
2 tsp Xanthan gum
½ tsp baking soda
⅓ cup currants or
   raisins
⅓ cup rolled oats

WARM the first 4 ingredients in a 3 qt. saucepan until honey melts.

COMBINE ¾ cup of oat flour with rice flour, baking powder, baking soda & gum.

STIR into oil mixture.

ADD currants and beat for 50 strokes.

ADD gradually, enough oat flour to make a dough that forms a ball that isn't sticky.

DIVIDE dough into 2 balls.

SCATTER ½ of the rolled oats on a board.

PLACE 1 ball on top and roll it to cover with oats.

FLATTEN into a 6" circle about 3⁄4" thick.

TURN to evenly coat with oats.

PLACE in an ungreased cookie sheet scattered
    with more oats.

CUT into 8 wedges, but do not separate wedges.

REPEAT with remaining dough and oats.

BAKE at 325° for 25 minutes, or until golden
    brown.

COOL for 30 minutes.

PLUM BREAKFAST PASTRY

You can make part of this the night before.

3⁄4 cup rice flour	1 cup non-dairy sour
3⁄4 cup bean flour	cream
2 tsp Xanthan gum	8-10 oz plum jam
1⁄2 tsp salt	2⁄3 cups chopped
1⁄2 cup mashed potatoes	walnuts
1 cup butter	1 cup coconut

COMBINE flours, potatoes, salt & Xanthan gum.

CUT in butter as for a pie crust.

MIX in non-dairy sour cream. ("Emo")

REFRIGERATE over night.

LET stand at room temperature for 1 hour.

CUT dough in half and roll each half into a
    10" x 15" rectangle.

SPREAD each with 1/2 of the jam, coconut and
    nuts.
ROLL up lengthwise, jellyroll style.

BAKE at 325° for 55 minutes. Cool.

SPRINKLE with powdered sugar and slice.

DUTCH BABIES

3 large eggs	3 tbl butter
6 tbl rice flour	powdered sugar
1 tbl granulated sugar	1 lemon in wedges
6 tbl milk or water	

MIX first 4 ingredients in processor until smooth.
    (Can be chilled overnight.)

PUT butter into 10"-12" fry pan and set pan in
    oven at 425°.

ADD batter when butter is melted.

BAKE until pancake puffs at edges - about 15
    minutes.

CUT into wedges and dust with sugar.

SQUEEZE on lemon juice.

❀ ❀ ❀ ❀

CINNAMON RAISIN COFFEE CAKE -
Sugar-free

⅓ ripe banana, mashed   1 ½ cup bean flour
½ cup butter or margarine 1 ½ cup rice flour
3 large eggs   1 tsp baking soda
1 tsp vanilla extract   4 tsp baking powder
1 ½ cup water   3 tsp Xanthan gum
                           1 ½ cup raisins

TOPPING
1⁄3 cup raisins or chopped dates
1⁄3 cup chopped walnuts (or sliced almonds)
1⁄3 cup flaked coconut
1 tsp cinnamon

MASH bananas with butter.

ADD eggs, extract, & water to mashed banana &
    butter.

BEAT.

MEASURE in flours, baking soda, baking powder,
    gum & raisins.

POUR into oiled and floured 9"x 13"" pan.

COMBINE topping and sprinkle over batter.

BAKE at 300° for 25 minutes.

BLUEBERRY MUFFINS

2⁄3 cup banana	1 tsp soda
1 egg	3 tsp baking powder
1 cup milk or water	2⁄3 cup rice flour
1⁄3 cup oil or shortening	2⁄3 cup bean flour

2 tsp Xanthan gum   1 cup blueberries
2⁄3 cup potato flour or mashed potato

MIX the first 4 ingredients. (Easier in a processor.)

SIFT dry ingredients. (potato or potato flour must
    be very well mixed)

ADD flour mixture to the egg mixture.

ADD blueberries.

POUR into muffin tins that have been oiled and
    floured.

FILL 3⁄4 full.

BAKE at 300° for 40 minutes.

MAKES 1 dozen.

If you do not have a banana, you may use 3 or 4
small canned yams (equal to 1 banana) plus 1⁄4
cup sugar.

Wonderfully moist...

PUMPKIN BREAD

1 1/2 cups bean flour
1 1/2 cups rice flour
1 1/2 tsp salt   1 cup corn oil
1 tsp ground cinnamon   1/2 cup water
1 tsp nutmeg   4 eggs
2 tsp baking soda
3 tsp Xanthan gum
2 cups pureed cooked or canned pumpkin
1 cup honey (2 1/3 cups sugar plus 2/3 cup water)

GREASE and flour 2 loaf pans.

STIR together in a large bowl, flour, sugar, baking
    soda, salt, and spices.

STIR together pumpkin, corn oil and water.

ADD eggs one at a time beating well.

MAKE a well in the center of the flour mixture.

ADD pumpkin mixture and stir.

POUR into prepared pans.

BAKE at 325° for 1 hour.

COOL for 10 minutes.

MAKES 2 loaves.

Dr. Green claimed not to like "being a guinea pig," but every last crumb of this bread disappeared!

ZUCCHINI BREAD

¾ cup rice flour
¾ cup bean flour
2 tsp Xanthan gum
½ tsp baking powder
½ tsp baking soda
½ tsp salt
1 tsp cinnamon

2 eggs
1⅓ cup sugar or
1 cup honey
½ cup chopped pecans
⅔ cup cooking oil
2 tsp vanilla
1⅓ cup shredded
   zucchini

Reducing the sugar to ½ cup brown sugar tastes
    less sweet, but cake will not raise as well.

SIFT together flour, gum, baking powder, baking
    soda, salt & cinnamon. Set aside.

BEAT eggs until blended.

GRADUALLY add sugar and oil, mixing well after
    each addition.

BLEND in vanilla.

STIR in zucchini and nuts.

ADD dry ingredients.

MIX until dry ingredients are just moistened.

POUR into greased 9"x 5"x 3"" loaf pan.

BAKE in 325° oven for 1 hour or until cake tester
    comes out clean.

TURN out on a rack to cool.

COOL for 10 minutes.

RICE BRAN BREAD

2 cups rice flour   4 egg yolks
1/2 cup soya or bean flour   2 cups buttermilk
21/2 tsp Xanthan gum   2 tbl salad oil
11/2 cups rice bran   1/2 cup molasses,
2 tbl baking powder   sugar or honey
1 tsp salt   4 egg whites
1 tsp soda   1/2 cup raisins
2 tbl potato flour

COMBINE the first 8 ingredients together.

ADD yolks, buttermilk, oil and sweetener.

BLEND well or at low speed until combined.

FOLD in stiffly beaten egg whites and raisins.

BAKE in 2 pans 8" x 4½" for 1 hour at 325°.

You can substitute water plus one more teaspoon baking powder for the buttermilk. Omit soda.

OLD FASHIONED INDIAN RYE BREAD

3 cups corn meal   1 ½ cups buttermilk
1 tsp salt   4 cups rye flour
½ cup molasses   2 tsp soda
1 cup water or milk   ½ cup stewed Irish potato

ADD salt and molasses to corn meal.

POUR boiling milk over it.

ADD cold buttermilk to rye flour and baking soda.
MIX all ingredients together.

ADD potato.

KNEAD until firm, then place in a round baking
    pan.

PLACE in 375° oven (without rising) and bake for
    2 hours.

PLACE pan of water in bottom of oven to help
    reduce browning and cover lightly with
    tinfoil.

WHEN done, cover with butter and a towel to
    retain moisture.

MAKES one loaf.

May add raisins. The very hard crust was to help
preserve the bread in the 1800's. If it is too tough
for you, use it for dunking. The flavor is great.

We know not to make a steady diet of deep-fried foods, but after tasting some of the fry bread of the Warm Spring Indians, I decided to make it with alternative flours. The best, most exciting bread was made with oat flour, but the bean flour came in a close second. The Warm Spring Indians served it with blackberry jam! Excellent!

INDIAN FRY BREAD

1½ cups oat (or bean) flour
1½ cups rice flour
1 tbl sugar
3 tsp Xanthan gum

2 tbl baking powder
2 tsp shortening
1 tsp salt
1½ cups cold water
oil

MIX dry ingredients.

CUT in shortening.

ADD enough water to make thick dough and knead well.

HEAT oil in deep fryer or Dutch oven to 350°.

BREAK off handfuls of dough and fry until golden brown.

DRAIN and serve warm.

OTHER BREAD-LIKE GOODIES

CROUTONS

SPREAD 2 slices of wheat-free bread with a thin
   layer of Dijon mustard on both sides.

CUT into small cubes and spread on waxed paper
   on a cookie tin.

MICROWAVE on high for 1½ minutes.

STIR well and MICROWAVE for another 1½
   minutes or until bread is dry to touch.

DUMPLINGS

1 cup Biscuit mix (p. 3)   ½ cup milk or water

STIR milk (water) into baking mix to form stiff
   dough.

DROP by spoonsful onto simmering stew, or soup.

COVER and cook 15 minutes.
                        Makes 5 large dumplings

OPTIONAL: ADD ¼ cup grated cheddar or

ADD 2 tsp dried parsley before adding liquid.

CORNMEAL DUMPLINGS

½ cup bean flour   ½ tsp salt
½ cup yellow cornmeal   2 tbl vegetable oil
1 tsp baking powder   ¼ cup milk or water
1 small onion finely   1 egg
  chopped
¼ tsp ground thyme (optional)

MIX all ingredients.

DROP by spoonfuls onto hot chicken broth or
    stew.

COVER and simmer for 20 minutes.

Also good with ham hocks.

*These crepes make a handy and flavorful substitute for a
sandwich as you can wrap them around almost any filling.*

FAUX CREPES

(You may substitute buckwheat, oat or amaranth
for the bean flour.)

1/2 cup bean flour   2/3 cup water
1/2 tsp salt   2 tsp olive oil
1/2 tsp Xanthan gum (or 1 egg)

SIFT flour gum and salt into mixing bowl.

ADD half the water. (and egg if used)

MIX with a whisk if difficult.

STIR in the rest of water and let rest for
      10 minutes.

HEAT non-stick 8"-9" skillet over medium high
      heat.

BRUSH lightly with olive oil (1 tsp).

When hot, POUR on all of batter and rotate pan to
      spread batter evenly. (batter should sizzle)

COOK for 2 minutes until brown at edges.

POUR on 1 tsp oil and cook 5 minutes more.

TURN crepe. (fingers best!)

COOK for 5 minutes and remove.

COVER with towel in 200° oven.

SERVE immediately.

SERVE with fruit or

> GARLIC BUTTER
> 6 tbl unsalted butter
> 1 garlic clove chopped
> WARM and pour over crepes

OPTIONAL: add parsley, basil or garlic powder to give a savory taste.

Now you can have Stroganoff again!

NOODLES

1¾ cups rice flour	4 whole eggs
1¾ cups bean flour	5 egg yolks
3 tsp Xanthan gum	1 tbl salt
or substitute	

2½ cup rice flour ⎫
⅔ cup potato starch ⎬   for the rice/bean flour
⅓ cup tapioca flour ⎭

ADD enough water, 1 tsp at a time, to mix dough
    into a ball.

COVER with tea towel and let rest for 45 minutes.

ROLL out very thin. Let rest for 20-30 minutes.

CUT into noodles by rolling up and slicing with a
        sharp knife or use a pasta or pizza cutter.

COOK in boiling water for 12-15 minutes.

DRAIN and add butter or 1 tbl of olive oil.

A pasta machine is a luxury, but gives a uniform
thickness and size to noodles, spaghetti or maca-
roni.

BUCKWHEAT SPAGHETTI

1 cup buckwheat flour   4 tbl water
4 tsp oil

COMBINE all ingredients to form a firm dough.

KNEAD for 10 minutes.

PLACE dough on an oiled surface and roll as
    thinly as possible.

CUT into fine strips. (a pasta maker works best)

COOK spaghetti for 3 minutes in boiling salted
    water with 1 tbl oil added.

DRAIN and serve with a sauce of your choice.

CRACKERS

2 cups amaranth, bean, oat or corn flour
1 tsp baking powder or soda
1 tsp salt
1/3 cup olive, safflower, corn or vegetable oil
About 2/3 cup cold water

MIX flour, baking powder or soda and salt.

ADD oil and mix with a fork until crumbly.

ADD water slowly, as needed.

FORM into 2 balls and chill.

ROLL out 1 ball to about 1/4" on lightly greased
   baking sheet.

SPRINKLE dough with flour if it sticks to rolling
   pin.

CUT into 2" squares.

PRICK several times with fork.

BAKE in preheated oven at 350° for 10 minutes or
   until brown.

WATCH CAREFULLY TO AVOID BURNING!

Save crumbs in a container in the freezer for
   breading, stuffings, etc.

ADD 1/2 teaspoon of a favorite seasoning.

(3 tbl of Amaranth flour has the calcium of 1/2 cup
   milk, but this flour is expensive.)

Nothing tastes as good as a fresh homemade tortilla!

CORN TORTILLAS

2 cups Masa Harina   1 cup water

COMBINE with hands till dough holds its shape.

ADD more water if necessary.

LET stand 15 minutes.

DIVIDE into 12 balls (about the size of golf balls).

DAMPEN dough slightly with water.

PRESS between sheets of waxed paper with
        rolling pin.

ROLL out to about 6 inches in diameter.

PLACE tortilla paperside up on <u>ungreased</u> griddle.

PEEL off paper and cook 30 seconds or until
        edges begin to dry.

TURN, cook until surface appears puffy and dry.

SPREAD with butter or fry in hot oil.

STORE in refrigerator for 2 weeks or freeze.

REHEAT in oven or microwave.
12 tortillas

CAKES

"...there is a longing for good foods
and tranquil surroundings..."

Cross Creek Kitchens
Sally Morrison

Sooner or later we all discover that the important moments in life are not the advertised ones, not the birthdays, the graduations, the weddings, not the great goals achieved. The real milestones are less prepossessing. They come to the door of memory unannounced, stray dogs that amble in, sniff around a bit, and simply never leave. Our lives are measured by these.

Susan B. Anthony
(grandniece of Susan B.)

(I remember the man who brings me eggs on Thursdays!)

a time saver...

CAKE MIX

4 cups rice flour	1 tbl salt
4 cups bean flour	8 tsp Xanthan gum
2 tbl baking soda	6 cups granulated sugar

COMBINE all ingredients in large bowl.

STIR until blended.

DIVIDE mixture into 6 individual packages.

STORE in a tightly sealed container in a cool dry
place.

MAKES about 6 cakes.

Use within 10 weeks.

VERY CHOCOLATE (SNACK) CAKE

2¼ cups cake mix	⅓ cup vegetable oil
2 tbl unsweetened cocoa	1 tsp vanilla
powder	½ cup semisweet
¾ cup water	chocolate chips
1 egg	½ cup chopped nuts

PREHEAT oven to 350°.

COMBINE cake mix and cocoa powder in an
     ungreased 8"-9" baking pan.

COMBINE water, egg, oil and vanilla in medium
     bowl.

STIR into cocoa mixture until smooth and blended.

SPRINKLE chocolate pieces and nuts evenly over
     batter.

BAKE 30-40 minutes at 350°.
                    9 servings

GINGERBREAD

2½ cups cake mix (p.35)   ½ cup butter or
4 tsp baking powder   margarine
1 tbl ginger   2 eggs
1 tsp cinnamon   1 cup water
¼ tsp cloves   ⅔ cup molasses

PREHEAT oven to 325°.

SIFT together dry ingredients in large mixing bowl.

MELT butter and beat with eggs and water.

ADD butter mixture to dry ingredients and stir well.

ADD molasses and stir well.

TURN into greased and floured 8"x 8"x 2"" pan.

BAKE for 60 minutes at 325°.

SERVE warm with whipped cream.

OLD TIME GINGERBREAD

½ cup brown sugar
½ cup lard or shortening
1 cup dark molasses
1 egg
1 tsp soda
1 tbl chocolate or cocoa

1 ⅛ cup rice flour
1 ⅛ cup bean flour
2 tsp Xanthan gum
½ tsp salt
1 tbl ginger
1cup boiling hot water

CREAM first 3 ingredients.

ADD beaten egg.

SIFT dry ingredients and add.

MIX well.

ADD hot water and mix again.

BAKE at 325° for 60-70 minutes in a large well-
    greased pan.

SPICE CAKE

¾ cup rolled oats   1 tsp ground cinnamon
1 ¼ cups boiling water   ½ tsp ground nutmeg
2¼ cups cake mix   1 tsp vanilla extract
    (see p. 35)   ½ cup chopped nuts
1 egg   ½ cup raisins
⅓ cup vegetable oil   coconut topping

PREHEAT oven to 350°.

COMBINE oats and boiling water and set aside.

COMBINE egg, oil, vanilla and spices.

STIR into softened rolled oats mixture.

STIR into cake mix.

ADD nuts and raisins and mix.

BAKE 45 minutes at 325°.

Broiled Coconut Topping is great on this cake.

🌹   🌹   🌹   🌹

So good on spice or ginger cake...

BROILED COCONUT TOPPING

4 tbl butter or margarine	½ tsp vanilla extract
¼ cup packed brown sugar	½ cup shredded coconut
2 tbl milk or water	½ cup chopped nuts

MELT butter in saucepan.

STIR in remaining ingredients.

SPREAD topping evenly over cake as it comes
     from the oven.

PLACE cake in oven 3" below broiling element.

BROIL about 2 minutes until bubbly.

9 servings

🌹   🌹   🌹   🌹

This is a wonderfully moist cake that freezes well.

FLOURLESS POUND CAKE

1 lb. (2 cups) sugar	10 egg yolks
1 lb. ground pecans	10 egg whites

GRIND nuts finely in the food processor or
blender.

BEAT egg yolks until they are lemon color & very
thick.

ADD sugar and nuts and stir until well mixed.

BEAT egg whites until stiff and fold ¼ of whites
into the nut mixture.

FOLD in the remaining whites very thoroughly.

POUR into a greased tube pan and bake at 250°-
300° for about 1 hour.

Good with whipped cream or non-dairy topping.

WHEAT-FREE CHOCOLATE CAKE

3 cups Biscuit mix (p. 3)	3 tbl cocoa
3⁄4 cup water	1 tsp vanilla
2 eggs	1 cup sugar

MIX and bake at 350° for 30 minutes.

CHOCOLATE PUDDING CAKE

1 cup biscuit mix	1⁄2 cup milk or water
1 cup granulated sugar	1 tsp vanilla
3 tbl unsweetened cocoa	1⁄3 cup unsweetened cocoa
	1⁄2 cup gran. sugar
	1 2⁄3 cups hot water

Confectioners sugar (optional)

MIX first 3 ingredients in greased 8" square baking dish.

STIR in milk and vanilla.

SPRINKLE 1⁄3 cup cocoa and 1⁄2 cup granulated sugar.

POUR on hot water.

BAKE in preheated 325° oven for 50 minutes or
until top is firm.

DUST with confectioners sugar.   6 servings.

❦   ❦   ❦   ❦

*Young son, Neal, made this cake for Dr. Harms, the veterinar-
ian, who loaned him a Hampshire "ram" to court the ladies in
his flock of sheep.*

PINEAPPLE UPSIDEDOWN CAKE

3 cups Biscuit mix (p. 3)   3 eggs, slightly beaten
1½ cups milk (or water)   1½ tsp vanilla
1⅓ cups sugar (or   1 20 oz can sliced
   1 cup honey)   pineapple, drained

Brown Sugar Topping
       1 cup brown sugar, firmly packed
       ½ cup butter or margarine

BUTTER a 13" x 9"" pan or 2 8" square pans.

PREPARE Brown Sugar Topping and pat into
       bottom of pan.

PLACE pineapple evenly over topping.

COMBINE biscuit mix and sugar in large bowl.

COMBINE milk, eggs and vanilla in a small bowl.

ADD half of milk mixture to dry ingredients.

BEAT 2 minutes until smooth.

ADD remaining milk mixture and beat 2-3 minutes.

SPREAD over pineapple.

BAKE 1 hour until center springs back when
    touched.

COOL for 10 minutes.

TURN out onto serving plate.

UPSIDEDOWN CAKE

Sliced fruit (pineapple,   2 tbl butter
    or peach or...)   1⁄4 tsp cinnamon
1⁄3 cup brown sugar   1⁄4 cup chopped nuts
1 tbl frozen orange juice concentrate
1 recipe shortcake batter (p. 44)

SPREAD sliced fruit in 8" x 8" baking pan.

MIX sugar and juice, spread over sliced fruit.

POUR shortcake mix over all.

BAKE at 350° for 25 minutes.

❧   ❧   ❧   ❧

SHORTCAKE

3 cups Biscuit mix (p. 3)   ½ cup water (or milk)
2 tbl sugar   1 egg, beaten
¼ cup butter or   fruit, whipped cream
  margarine

PREHEAT oven to 375°.

COMBINE Biscuit mix and sugar in medium bowl.

COMBINE melted butter, water and egg.

ADD to dry ingredients with fork until just
        moistened.

KNEAD 8-10 times on lightly-floured surface.

ROLL out dough to ¾" thickness.

CUT with lightly floured cutter.

BAKE on unbuttered baking sheet about 20
        minutes until browned.

OR
ADD 1/2 cup additional water.

POUR dough into 8" square baking pan.

BAKE about 20 minutes until browned.

CUT into six shortcake pieces.

Especially good in your Cinnamon Raisin Stuffing...if there is any left over!

EGGLESS, MILKLESS, BUTTERLESS CAKE

2 cups brown sugar	1 tsp soda
2 cups hot water	1 tsp cinnamon
2 tbl shortening	1 tsp cloves
1 tsp salt	1 1/2 cups rice flour
1 pkg seedless raisins,	1 1/2 cups bean flour
(1 cup)	3 tsp Xanthan gum

BOIL together the first 5 ingredients.

COOL.

WHEN cold, add flour and soda dissolved in a tsp
    hot water.

DIVIDE into 2 greased loaf pans.

BAKE about 45 minutes at 325°.
   Will keep moist for quite some time.

Ed's secretary brought this recipe into the bank one day. It's awfully good! (I changed the wheat part.)

CARROT CAKE

¾ cup bean flour
¾ cup rice flour
½ cup potato flour
   or increase rice flour
2 tsp Xanthan gum
2 tsp soda
½ tsp salt
2 tsp cinnamon
¼ tsp nutmeg

1½ cups cooking oil
4 eggs
1½ cups honey
2 cups grated carrots
1 small can crushed
   pineapple,well-drained
1 cup chopped walnuts
1 tsp vanilla

MIX together dry ingredients.

BEAT oil, honey & eggs for 3 minutes.

ADD to flour mixture.

ADD remaining ingredients.

BAKE in a 9" x13"" pan for 65-70 minutes at 325°.

FROSTING
   4 oz cream cheese, softened.
   1⁄4 cup butter
   2 tsp fresh lemon juice or frozen orange
      juice concentrate
   1⁄2 tsp grated lemon or orange
   3⁄4 cups powdered sugar.

SPREAD on cool cake.

*This wonderful cake won a first place ribbon at the Clackamas
County Fair in the summer of 1990. I was thrilled! The
addition of vegetables such as squash, pumpkin, carrots, etc.
gives moistness and structure to a wheat-free cake.*

CHOCOLATE ZUCCHINI CAKE

1 cup rice flour   3⁄4 cup soft butter
1 1⁄4 cup bean flour   2 cups sugar
2 tsp Xanthan gum   3 eggs
1⁄2 cup cocoa   2 tsp vanilla
1 tbl baking powder   2 tsp orange peel
1 1⁄2 tsp soda   2 cup shredded zucchini
1 tsp salt   1⁄2 cup milk or water
1 tsp cinnamon   1 cup chopped nuts

COMBINE first 8 ingredients and set aside.

CREAM butter and sugar.

ADD eggs one at a time, and vanilla, orange peel
     and zucchini.

STIR in, alternately, flour mixture and milk.

ADD nuts.

POUR batter into greased & floured tube pan or
     loaf pan.

BAKE at 325° for about 1 1/2 hours.

COOL with oven door open for 30 minutes.

TURN out and cool completely.

FROST if desired.

AUSTRIAN CAKES

2 tbl butter or margarine
5 eggs, separated (room temp.)
pinch salt
1 tsp vanilla extract
2 tsp granulated sugar

1/3 cup confec-
tioners' sugar
1/4 cup rice flour
2 tbl cream
sherry

PREHEAT oven to 350°.

MELT butter in 10" shallow baking dish or oven-
proof skillet.

BEAT egg whites in medium bowl just until they
form peaks.

SPRINKLE with 2 tsp granulated sugar.

BEAT until whites are stiff but not dry.

BEAT egg yolks in a large bowl with confectioners
sugar for about 1 minute.

STIR flour, vanilla, sherry and 1/4 of egg whites
into yolk mixture.

FOLD in remaining whites gently.

COAT bottom of baking dish with melted butter.

SPOON 6 mounds egg mixture into baking dish.

BAKE 10-12 minutes until lightly browned and still
     slightly soft inside.

SPRINKLE with 1 tsp granulated sugar.
     6 servings.

*This torte was brought in on a Monday to the folks in the
Library at work. I wanted them to be guinea pigs. I also
wanted to cheer them up because they couldn't be outside in the
beautiful sunshine. Did they think this dessert was good
enough to substitute for a wheat cake on someone's special
occasion? They thought it was.*

TOO BAD IT'S MONDAY CAKE
(Toffee Meringue)

9 egg white
1 tsp vanilla
1 tsp white vinegar
1¾ cps powdered sugar
1 pt whipping cream or
  non-dairy whipped
  topping

4 chocolate-covered
  toffee bars (Skor or
  Heath - 1¼ oz ea)
Garnish with 2 more
  toffee bars

HEAT oven to 275°.

BEAT egg whites with electric mixer until soft
      peaks form.
BEAT in vanilla and vinegar until well blended.

GRADUALLY add sugar, beating till peaks are stiff
      and glossy.
LINE 1 or 2 baking sheets with brown paper.

TRACE 2 9" circles on the paper.

SPREAD meringue mixture over 2 circles.

BAKE 1 hour. Turn off heat. DO NOT OPEN
      OVEN!
LET stand in oven for 2 hours or until cool.

ASSEMBLE right away when cool.

WHIP cream with electric mixer until soft peaks
      form. (You will have 4 cups of whipped
      cream.)
PUT 1/2 of whipped cream in separate bowl.

FOLD chopped toffee into one bowl.

REMOVE 1 meringue from pan to serving plate.

SPREAD wirh candy mixture.

REMOVE 2nd meringue layer and place on top.

SPREAD with plain whipped cream.

GARNISH with candy pieces.

REFRIGERATE 8 hours or overnight.
12 servings

❀   ❀   ❀   ❀

This wonderful dessert easily takes the place of a birthday or special occasion cake.

LEMON TORTE

4 egg whites
1 tsp vanilla
1/2 tsp cream of tartar
3/4 cp sugar
2 tbl sliced almonds
2/3 cps sugar
1 tsp unflavored gelatin

6 beaten egg yolks
1/2 tsp grated lemon
   peel
1/3 cp lemon juice
2 tbl margerine
1/3 cp water
3/4 cp whipping cream
   or non-dairy topping

BEAT first 3 ingredients with an electric mixer till
soft peaks form.

ADD, gradually, sugar until peaks are stiff.

LINE 2 or 3 baking sheets with brown paper.

TRACE 3 circles each about 7" across on the
    paper.

SPREAD meringue mixture over the 3 circles.

SPRINKLE the almonds over one circle to form
    the top layer.

BAKE in 300° oven for 45 minutes.

TURN off oven. DO NOT OPEN THE DOOR.

ALLOW meringues to dry in the oven for 3 hours
    or overnight.

COMBINE in sauce pan, the 2/3 cp sugar and
    gelatin.

ADD yolks, lemon peel, juice, margarine, and
    water.

COOK and stir till bubbly.

COOK for 2 minutes more.

REMOVE from heat and cover surface with waxed
    paper.

COOL.

CHILL till mixture becomes more firm.

WHIP cream till soft peaks form.

ADD whipped cream (or non-dairy whipped topping) to lemon mixture.

PUT one meringue on a platter.

SPREAD half of lemon mixture over it.

PLACE second meringue on top.

SPREAD second half of lemon mixture over it.

PLACE the meringue with almonds on top.

COVER with a very loose piece of plastic wrap.

CHILL for 6 hours or overnight.

May serve with a fruit sauce such as the following:
    1 1/2 cup berries   2 tbl sugar
    1 tbl cornstarch

COOK until bubbly for 2 minutes.

COVER and chill.

This filling is so simple and so good! The Australians call the finished meringue dessert, 'Pavlova,' in honor of the celebrated ballerina, Anna Pavlova.

KIWI FILLING

1 cup chilled whipping cream
2 tbl sugar
    or
1 cup chilled non-dairy whipped topping
3 kiwis, peeled and sliced

BEAT whipping cream and sugar until stiff.

FROST top and sides of the meringue (p. 56).

ARRANGE kiwi slices on top.

1½ - 2 cups fresh strawberries, raspberries or blueberries can be substituted for the kiwis.

MERINGUE

3 egg whites   1/4 tsp cream of tartar
1/2 tsp vanilla   3/4 cup sugar

PREHEAT oven to 225°.

LINE bottom of cookie sheet with brown paper.

TRACE a circle about 8 or 9 inches in diameter.

BEAT egg whites and cream of tartar until foamy.

ADD vanilla.

BEAT in 3/4 cup sugar, 1 tbl at a time until stiff.

SPREAD within the circle you drew in the pan.

BAKE 1 1/2 hours. Turn off oven.

DO NOT OPEN OVEN for 3 hours.

SPREAD on filling when cool.

CUT into wedges to serve.

Oldest son, Harvey doesn't like to be fooled! "Are these wheat-free?" he asks. "You tell me!" answers Mom.

BROWNIES

2 squares unsweetened chocolate
        or 6 tbl cocoa plus 2 tbl shortening
1⁄4 cup butter or margarine

MIX over hot water or low heat or MICROWAVE
      for 30 seconds.

REMOVE from heat.

STIR in
            1 cup sugar   1⁄4 cup rice flour
            2 unbeaten eggs   1⁄2 cup walnuts,
            1⁄8 tsp salt   chopped
            1⁄4 cup bean flour   1 tsp vanilla
            1 tsp Xanthan gum

BAKE until dry on top and almost firm to touch at
      325° for 35 minutes.

COOL

CUT into bars.

If you really LIKE brownies...

BROWNIE MIX

4½ cups rice flour   8 cups sugar
1½ cups soy or bean flour   1 (8 oz) can
8 tsp baking powder   unsweetened cocoa
4 tsp salt   2 cups shortening
6 tsp Xanthan gum

SIFT together flour, baking powder, salt and
    Xanthan gum.

ADD sugar and cocoa.

CUT in shortening with pastry blender.

PUT in a large airtight container. LABEL!

STORE in a cool dry place. Use within 10 weeks.

MAKES 17 cups of mix.

From the Brownie mix...

WONDERFUL BROWNIES

2 eggs, beaten	⅓ cup water
1 tsp vanilla	½ cup chopped nuts
2 ½ cups Brownie mix	

PREHEAT to 350°.

GREASE and flour an 8" square pan.

COMBINE eggs, vanilla and Brownie mix.

BEAT until smooth.

STIR in nuts. (nuts sprinkled on top before baking looks nice)

POUR into prepared pan.

BAKE for 1 hour at 325°.

COOL. CUT into 2 inch bars.

MISSISSIPPI MUD

4 eggs	2 cups chopped nuts
1/2 cup margarine	1 cup flaked coconut
3 cups Brownie mix	7 oz marshmallow creme
1 tsp vanilla	chocolate icing

PREHEAT oven to 325°.

GREASE and flour 13" x 9"" baking pan.

BEAT eggs until foamy.

ADD melted margarine.

ADD Brownie mix and blend well.

STIR in vanilla, nuts and coconut.

POUR into prepared pan.

BAKE about 30 minutes, until edges separate from
    pan.

SPREAD on marshmallow creme while still hot.

FROST with chocolate icing.

CHOCOLATE ICING

COMBINE 1/2 cup melted butter, 6 tbl water & 4 tbl
cocoa.

ADD to 1 lb. powdered sugar.

BEAT until smooth.

APPLECAKE

2 cups coarsely grated apples 1/4 cup oil
3/4 cup honey (1 cup sugar)   1/2 cup raisins
1/2 tsp salt   1 cup chopped nuts
1 tsp soda   3/4 cup rice flour
1 tsp cinnamon   3/4 cup bean flour
1/2 tsp nutmeg   1 tsp Xanthan gum

MIX and BAKE at 325° for 60 minutes in 8" square
greased pan.

APPLESAUCE CAKE

3⁄4 cup bean flour
3⁄4 cup rice flour
1 1⁄2 tsp Xanthan gum
1 cup sugar
1 tsp soda
1⁄2 tsp salt
1⁄2 tsp cinnamon

1⁄4 tsp nutmeg
1⁄8 tsp cloves
1 tbl vinegar
6 tbl vegetable oil
1 tsp vanilla
3⁄4 cup applesauce
1⁄4 cup cold water

MIX and BAKE at 350° for 25 minutes in 8" square
   greased pan.

*This recipe is a family tradition. I make it every fall, all the
while remembering "It's fruitcake weather," from Truman
Capote's story, A Christmas Memory.*

DARK FRUIT CAKE

1 1⁄2 lb raisins
1 lb. citron, orange or lemon peel
3-4 lbs glaced fruit
1⁄2 lb dates
2 cups chopped apple
1 lb walnuts
2 1⁄2 cups rice flour
2 1⁄2 cup bean flour
5 tsp Xanthan gum

7 eggs
12 oz jar jelly
1 tbl cinnamon
1 tbl allspice
1 tsp cloves
1 tsp nutmeg
3 tsp baking
       powder
1⁄2 tsp soda

1 cup butter
2 cups brown sugar

½ cup molasses
1 tbl rum extract
2 tsp vanilla

SET aside enough candied fruits for decorating
    cake tops.

CUT remaining fruits and nuts into small pieces
    and

DREDGE in 2 cups flour.

CREAM butter and sugar.

SEPARATE eggs and add one yolk at a time.
    (reserve whites)

BEAT until smooth.

BLEND in jelly. (I use apple or grape)

SIFT remaining flour with spices, baking powder,
    soda and Xanthan gum.

ADD to butter mixture.

ADD extracts and syrup and mix well.

ADD fruits to butter mixture.

BEAT egg whites until stiff but not dry.

FOLD into two 10" tube pans which have been greased and lined with paper.

BAKE at 250° for 3½ - 4 hours.

NOTE: To avoid excessive browning, use heavy brown paper liner and a pan of water on the bottom of the oven.

DONE when a cake tester is moist but not doughy.

BRUSH with syrup and decorate with candied fruit about 30 minutes after cake is done.

Fruitcakes should be cooled in the pan.

Thanks to instructor, Jan Anderson, who gave me this wonderful recipe, Emily's RICE CAKES started me experimenting with rice and other non-wheat flours.

Emily Dickinson's RICE CAKES

In 1851 Emily wrote Sue Gilbert, then teaching in Baltimore, mentioning how happy she was to send rice cakes to her friend.

½ cup butter
1 cup powdered sugar
2 eggs
1 cup rice flour
1 spoonful milk with ¼ tsp baking soda
flavor to suit (1 tsp mace and/or nutmeg)

CREAM butter.

BEAT eggs in a separate bowl.

ADD sugar to butter.

ADD eggs gently.

ADD remaining ingredients.

BAKE in an 8" round pan at 350° for 15-20
minutes.

"Rice cakes were usually saved to serve a guest
who dropped in for tea. At 'handed teas,' everyone sat down as platters of food were passed.
Such bounty sometimes served as supper." 1.

1. Emily Dickinson Profile of the Poet as Cook,
   Brose, Nancy Harris, 1946.

I would NEVER buy a doughnut maker if I could just eat a store-bought doughnut, but it is wonderful to know you can indulge and no "fat" is involved with the new teflon products.

DOUGHNUTS

USE above rice cake batter. (good idea to double
    the batter!)

ADD ½ cup water to batter.

FILL doughnut maker ¾ full of batter.

CLOSE for 5-7 minutes.

Doubling the batter will make 14 doughnuts.

Wonderful if frosted and dipped in chopped nuts!!

These donuts are wonderfully good! If you have to substitute for the buttermilk, the donuts will be denser, heavier, but still very tasty. They must be started a day in advance.

SINFULLY GOOD DONUTS

2 eggs   1½ cup bean flour
1 cup granulated sugar   1½ cup rice flour
2 medium potatoes,   3 tsp Xanthan gum

mashed to make 1 cup
5 tbl melted lard
1 cup buttermilk (or 1 cup soft tofu, liquified in blender)
2 tsp vanilla extract

3 tsp baking powder
1 1/2 tsp grated nutmeg
1 tsp baking soda
2 1/4 tsp cream of tartar
1/2 tsp salt
Confectioners' sugar
2 qts vegetable oil

BEAT eggs until frothy.

ADD sugar and blend well.

STIR in potatoes, lard, buttermilk and vanilla.

SIFT dry ingredients and add to potato mixture.

MIX just until flour is completely moistened.

COVER dough and refrigerate overnight.

PREHEAT oil in fryer or Dutch oven to 370° F.

ROLL out half the dough on a heavily floured surface until 1/2 inch thick.

REFRIGERATE the other half.

CUT out donuts with a heavily floured donut cutter. (pineapple cutter works, too)

SLIDE donuts into hot fat with a metal spatula and
      cook until golden brown on underside. (1-2
      minutes)
TURN carefully and fry for another minute.

TAKE from fat and drain on paper towels.

FRY donut holes and drain.

When cool, shake donuts in a paper sack with
      confectioners' sugar.

Donuts store better unsugared.
      makes 24 donuts

*Although this is wheat-free, it is not dairy-free. There is no
substitute for real cheese.*

ALMOND CHEESECAKE

1½ cups Quaker Oats,   ½ cup granulated sugar
   Quick or Old Fashioned, 1 tsp almond extract
   uncooked   3 eggs
½ cup finely chopped   2 cups sour cream
   almonds   2 tbl granulated sugar
⅓ cup packed brown sugar
⅓ cup margarine, melted
16 oz cream cheese, softened

PREHEAT oven to 350°.

GREASE bottom and sides of 9" springform pan.

COMBINE first four ingredients and mix well.

PRESS firmly onto bottom and up 1½" sides of
    pan.

BAKE 18 minutes. Cool.

BEAT cheese, sugar and ½ tsp extract at medium
    speed of mixer until fluffy.

ADD eggs, one at a time, beating well after each.

STIR in 1 cup sour cream.

POUR into prepared crust.

BAKE 50 minutes or until center is set.

MIX remaining sour cream, extract and granulated
    sugar and spread over cheesecake..

CONTINUE baking 10 minutes.

LOOSEN cake from rim of pan, cool and remove
    rim.

CHILL.

May garnish with whipped cream, orange and
      almonds.

                    serves 16

          ❀   ❀   ❀   ❀

I am indebted to Audrey Sinner for this deliciously moist cake.

OATMEAL CAKE

1¼ cup boiling water   1 tsp vanilla
1 cup rolled oats (uncooked,   1½ cup oat flour
    regular or quick)   1 tsp Xanthan gum
½ cup margarine   ½ tsp salt
1 cup granulated sugar   1 tsp soda
1 cup packed brown sugar   ¾ tsp cinnamon
2 eggs   ¼ tsp nutmeg

PREHEAT oven at 350°.

POUR boiling water over oats, cover and let stand
      for 20 minutes.

BEAT butter, gradually adding sugars, until fluffy.

BLEND in extract and eggs.

ADD oat mixture and mix well.

MIX together flour, gum, soda, salt, cinnamon and
    nutmeg.

ADD to creamed mixture and mix well.

POUR batter into well-greased pan.

BAKE in 350° for 50-55 minutes.

DO NOT REMOVE from the pan.

SPREAD coconut/nut frosting over cake while still
    warm.

FROSTING for Oatmeal Cake

1⁄4 cup margarine or butter, melted
1⁄2 cup firmly packed brown sugar
3 tbl water
1⁄3 cup chopped nuts
3⁄4 cup shredded or flaked coconut

COMBINE all ingredients.

SPREAD evenly over cake.

BROIL until frosting becomes bubbly.

PIES

Luckily, it's the GOOD tastes one remembers best!

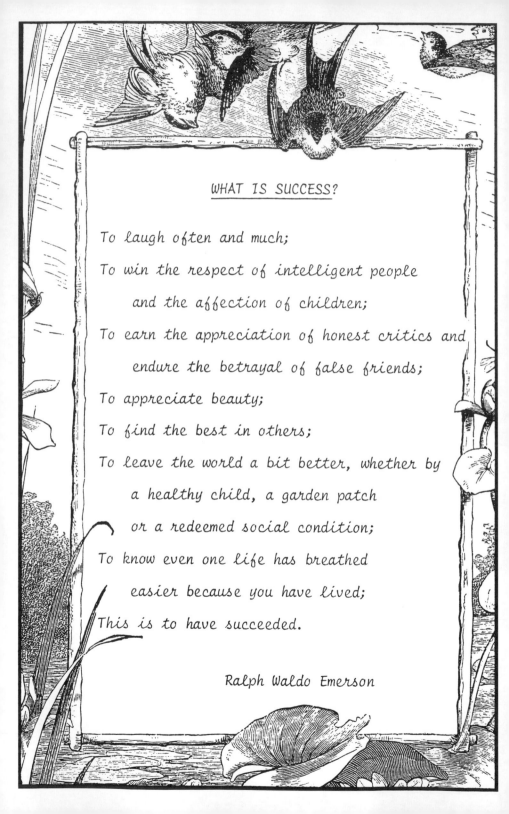

WHAT IS SUCCESS?

To laugh often and much;

To win the respect of intelligent people
    and the affection of children;

To earn the appreciation of honest critics and
    endure the betrayal of false friends;

To appreciate beauty;

To find the best in others;

To leave the world a bit better, whether by
    a healthy child, a garden patch
    or a redeemed social condition;

To know even one life has breathed
    easier because you have lived;

This is to have succeeded.

Ralph Waldo Emerson

It's so nice to have rolls of pie crust in your freezer. A delicious pie is not such an overwhelming task then.

PIE CRUST MIX

8 1/2 cups bean flour   2 tbl salt
8 1/2 cups white rice flour 1 (3lb) can shortening
6 tbl Xanthan gum   2 1/2 cups cold water

COMBINE flours, Xanthan gum and salt.

MIX with a pastry blender.

CUT in shortening and mix until particles are the
        size of peas.

ADD cold water and mix gently just enough to
        dampen entire mix.

IF mix is too sticky, sprinkle a little flour over all.

DIVIDE dough into 10 oblong rolls.

WRAP rolls separately in plastic wrap.

FREEZE. Makes enough for 10 double crust pies.

The Xanthan gum is vital to the manageability of
the dough. I recommend that you buy a pastry
cloth and roller cover.

DOUBLE PIE CRUST

THAW dough by leaving in refrigerator overnight
or by barely thawing in your microwave.

DIVIDE roll into 2 sections.

ROLL out on lightly floured pastry cloth to desired
thickness.

ROLL dough around the rolling pin to transfer to
your pie pan.

FILL and cover with the 2nd section.

PRESS and flute the edges.

BAKE according to directions.

SINGLE PIE CRUST

PREHEAT oven to 400°.

ROLL out 1/2 roll of pastry to desired thickness.

TRANSFER to your pie pan.

BAKE 15 minutes or until lightly browned. COOL!

If you haven't any pastry dough, and you need a pie NOW, here's a recipe for 1 pie.

DOUBLE PIE CRUST

1 cup rice flour   1/2 tsp salt
1 cup bean flour   3/4 cup vegetable shortening
2 tsp Xanthan gum   1/3 cup cold water

MIX with a pastry blender.

CUT in shortening and mix until particles are the
          size of peas.
ADD cold water and mix gently just enough to
          dampen entire mix.
IF mix is too sticky, sprinkle a little flour over all.

DIVIDE dough into 2 rolls.

ROLL out on lightly floured pastry cloth to desired
          thickness.
ROLL dough around the rolling pin to transfer to
          your pie pan.
FILL and cover with 2nd roll.

PRESS and flute the edges.

BAKE according to directions.

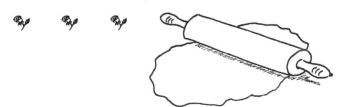

Square dancer, Marjorie Jacobs, taught me that microwaving the filling cuts down on baking time. Another hint is to brush the bottom crust with egg white before filling to keep the crust from getting soggy, and it makes the top crust look and taste great. These fruit pies even freeze well.

APPLE PIE

6-8 tart apples (6 cups)
1/2 cup honey (1/4 - 1 cup sugar)
3 tbl cornstarch (1 tbl with older apples)
1 tsp cinnamon
dash salt
1 recipe pie pastry

If apples are not tart, add 1 tbl lemon juice or
        grated lemon peel. For older apples, use
        more seasoning.

MIX AND MICROWAVE on high for 4 minutes
        stirring after 2 minutes.

POUR into 9" pie shell. Dot with butter and cover
        with crust.

BAKE at 350° for 40 minutes.

If you skip the MICROWAVE step, increase baking
        time to 1 hour.

MARIONBERRY PIE
(or Boysenberry)

3/4 cup honey (or 1 cup sugar)
3-4 tbl cornstarch   1 recipe pie pastry
4 cups berries   1 tbl butter or margarine

MIX cornstarch with berries.

POUR honey over berries and MICROWAVE 3-5
     minutes.

POUR into 10' pie shell, dot with butter and cover
     with crust.

BAKE 375° for 30 minutes or until brown.

If you skip the MICROWAVE step, increase baking
     time to 1 hour.

PEACH PIE

1 cup brown sugar
4 tbl cornstarch (or wheat-free flour)
Dash salt
6 cups fresh sliced peaches
1 tbl butter or margarine
1/4 tsp almond extract

MIX sugar, cornstarch (or flour) and salt in a large
    bowl.

STIR in fruit & MICROWAVE on high for 3-5
    minutes.

POUR into 10" pastry-lined pan.

DOT with butter and cover with crust.

BAKE at 350° for 40 minutes.

If you skip the MICROWAVE step, increase baking
    time to 1 hour.

60 SECOND BLUEBERRY PIE

2 cups fresh or dry pack frozen blueberries
1 15 oz can of blueberry pie filling
1/4 tsp almond extract
juice from 1/2 lemon and 1 tbl grated lemon rind

GENTLY fold in berries with pie filling.

ADD extract, juice and grated lemon.

POUR into prebaked pie shell and chill until ready
    to serve.

GARNISH with a ring of whipped topping.

BING CHERRY PIE (sweet cherry)

PREPARE crust for 10" pie.

FILL crust with cherries.

ADD 2-3 tbl tapioca   1 tsp lemon
    1/2 cup brown sugar   Dot with butter

BAKE at 350° for 40 minutes or until crust is nicely
    browned.

CHERRY COBBLER

1 cup cold water	1 lb sweet cherries
2 tbl cornstarch	1/4-1/3 cup sugar
1/4 tsp cinnamon	1 recipe shortcake batter
1/4 tsp salt	1/2 tsp almond extract

MIX water and cornstarch.

ADD rest of the ingredients.

BOIL for 5 minutes.

POUR into greased baking dish.

POUR Biscuit mix shortcake batter or Emily's Rice
Cake batter over all. (p. 44 or p. 64)

BAKE 350° for 20 minutes.

PEACH COBBLER

Substitute 1 pound of sliced peaches for cherries.

BERRY COBBLER

3 cups berries (boysenberry is great!)
sugar to taste (1/2 cup for boysenberries)
few grains salt
1 tbl bean or rice flour (or cornstarch)

MIX and spread in a buttered 8" x 8" baking dish.

DOT with butter or margarine.

SPREAD rice cake batter or short cake batter over
      the top. (p. 64 or p. 44)

BAKE at 350° for 20-25 minutes.

OLD FASHIONED PUMPKIN PIE

3 eggs	1/4 tsp salt
2/3 cup brown sugar	1/4 tsp ginger
3/4 cup water or milk	1/4 tsp nutmeg
1 1/2 cup cooked, drained,	1/4 tsp cloves
mashed pumpkin	1 tbl hot water

BEAT eggs till light and creamy.

STIR in sugar, water and pumpkin.

MIX spices with hot water and add.

POUR into 8" pastry-lined pan.

BAKE at 425° for 15 minutes.

REDUCE heat to 300° for 40 minutes or until
   custard is set.

IMPOSSIBLE PUMPKIN PIE

3/4 cup sugar	2 eggs
1/2 cup Biscuit mix (p. 3)	2 cups pumpkin (16 oz)
2 tbl butter or margarine	2 1/2 tsp pumpkin pie
13 oz evaporated milk	spice or 2 tsp allspice
or non-dairy creamer.	2 tsp vanilla

HEAT oven to 350°.

GREASE pie pan (9" or 10")

BEAT ingredients until smooth - 1 minute in
     blender on high or 2 minutes by hand.

POUR into pie plate.

BAKE until knife inserted in center comes out
     clean. 50-60 minutes.

CHOCOLATE IMPOSSIBLE PIE

1/2 cup Biscuit mix (p. 3) 4 tbl cocoa
1/2 cup sugar   1 tsp vanilla
4 eggs   1 tsp almond extract
2 cups milk (water)   1 tsp cinnamon
3 tbl soft butter or   1 cup flake coconut
   margarine

PREHEAT oven to 325°.

GREASE 9" round baking pan.

COMBINE all ingredients except coconut in
      processor or blender.

PROCESS for 1 minute.

POUR into the pan.

SPRINKLE coconut on top.

BAKE 40-45 minutes at 325°.

REMOVE to a rack to cool.

CHILL.
              Makes 8 servings.

IMPOSSIBLE FRENCH APPLE

6 cups sliced, peeled apples   3/4 cup milk or water
1 1/4 tsp ground cinnamon   1/2 cup Biscuit mix *
1/4 tsp nutmeg   2 eggs
1 cup brown sugar   2 tbl butter or
       margarine

Streusel topping:
2/3 cup Biscuit mix   2 tbl butter or margarine
1/2 cup nuts   1/4 cup brown sugar

HEAT to 325°.

GREASE 10" pie plate.

MIX apples and spices and pour into pie plate.

BEAT remaining ingredients except streusel until
      smooth (15 seconds in food processor,
      1 minute by hand)

SPRINKLE pie with streusel.

BAKE until knife inserted in center comes out
      clean, 55-60 minutes.

* Biscuit mix on p. 3

LEMON MERINGUE PIE

If you like a softer filling, reduce the flour and cornstarch.

4 tbl cornstarch	1 tbl butter or
4 tbl rice flour	margarine
1/2 tsp salt	1/4 tsp grated lemon
1 1/2 cups sugar	1/3 cup lemon juice
1 1/2 cups boiling water	4 egg yolks (save
	whites)

PREPARE and cool a 9" pie shell.

MIX first 4 ingredients in top of double boiler.

ADD boiling water.

COOK and stir over direct heat until mixture boils.

SET over hot water, cover and cook 20 minutes.

ADD rest of ingredients.

COOK and stir until thick.

COOL. (most important!)

MAKE meringue using the 4 egg whites. (p. 89)

POUR cooled lemon mixture into prepared pie
    shell.

SPOON meringue on top, spreading to touch
    edges.

BAKE at 425° until lightly browned. (5 minutes)

FOOLPROOF MERINGUE

1 tbl corn starch	1/4 tsp cream of tartar
2 tbl cold water	4 egg whites
1/2 cup boiling water	1/3 cup sugar

MIX together cornstarch and cold water in small
    saucepan.

STIR in boiling water.

COOK over medium heat stirring constantly until
    thickened - about 2 minutes.

REMOVE from heat and COOL. (very important -
    the cooling!)

ADD cream of tartar to egg whites.

BEAT until soft peaks form.

ADD sugar gradually, and continue beating.

ADD cornstarch mixture all at once.

BEAT until well-blended.

SPREAD over pie.

BAKE meringue in preheated oven at 425° for
      10-12 minutes until golden brown.

BERRY CRISP

4 cups blueberries (or apples, or peaches with
   cinnamon)
1/3 cup sugar
2 tsp lemon juice with berries
4 tbl butter or margarine (1/2 cup)
2/3 cup brown sugar
2/3 cup oat or rice flour
1 1/2 cup quick oats

PUT berries in deep greased baking dish.

SPRINKLE with white sugar and lemon juice.

CREAM butter and brown sugar.

ADD flour and oats.

SPREAD over berries.

BAKE 40 minutes at 375°.
           or
MICROWAVE for 15 minutes on high.

A combination of pears (3 cups) and cranberries
        (1 cup) is a very good option.

*Grandma Irene is famous for this recipe. She is often invited to
dinner with the request to bring an...*

APPLE CHARLOTTE

5 or 6 green cooking apples, sliced
1/2 cup raisins
1/4 cup brown sugar
1/4 cup granulated sugar
1 tsp cinnamon
1 double pie crust

SPREAD thin layer of butter or shortening over
        the bottom only of 2 qt. casserole dish

SPRINKLE thin layer of brown sugar over bottom.

LINE the dish with a layer of pastry as you would a
     pie dish.

FILL the baking dish with the apples.

ADD raisins, sugars and cinnamon.

DOT with 5 little dabs of "Crisco" or shortening.

COVER with 2nd layer of pastry.

BAKE 1 hour, 20 minutes at 325° till top is
     browned.

TURN upside down on plate <u>at once.</u>

Grandma Irene got this recipe from her mother...
Great Grandmother Nettie Weil - 1869-1945

COOKIES

Only in the part of us that we share, can we under-
stand each other.

Anonymous

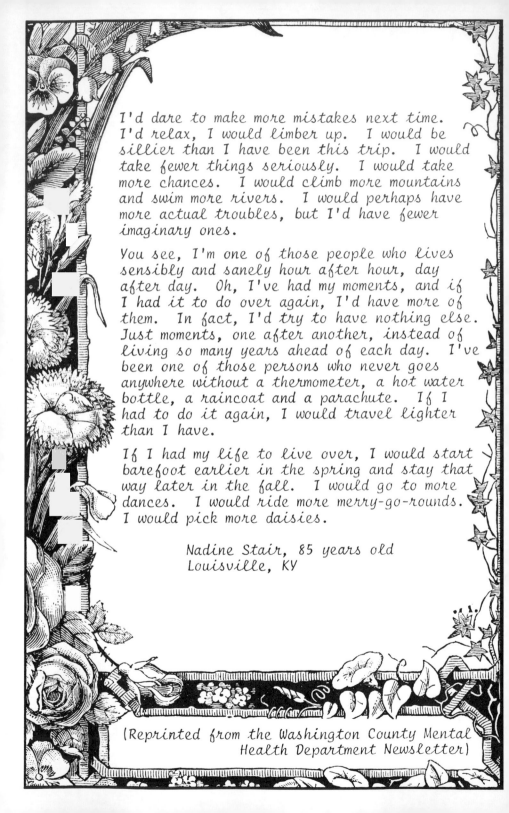

I'd dare to make more mistakes next time. I'd relax, I would limber up. I would be sillier than I have been this trip. I would take fewer things seriously. I would take more chances. I would climb more mountains and swim more rivers. I would perhaps have more actual troubles, but I'd have fewer imaginary ones.

You see, I'm one of those people who lives sensibly and sanely hour after hour, day after day. Oh, I've had my moments, and if I had it to do over again, I'd have more of them. In fact, I'd try to have nothing else. Just moments, one after another, instead of living so many years ahead of each day. I've been one of those persons who never goes anywhere without a thermometer, a hot water bottle, a raincoat and a parachute. If I had to do it again, I would travel lighter than I have.

If I had my life to live over, I would start barefoot earlier in the spring and stay that way later in the fall. I would go to more dances. I would ride more merry-go-rounds. I would pick more daisies.

Nadine Stair, 85 years old
Louisville, KY

(Reprinted from the Washington County Mental Health Department Newsletter)

WONDERFUL SUGAR COOKIES

1 cup butter or margarine
1 1⁄2 sugar (1 cup honey)
2 eggs
1 tsp vanilla

1 1⁄4 cups rice flour
1 cups bean flour
1⁄2 tsp salt
1 tsp baking powder
3 tsp Xanthan gum

CREAM butter and sugar.

ADD eggs and vanilla.

SIFT dry ingredients and add to butter mixture.

CHILL for 1 hour or more.

ADD enough flour to roll out.

CUT into desired shapes.

BAKE at 375° for 8 minutes.
                    Makes 30 cookies.

Husband, Ed, says these are the best I make!

TOLL HOUSE COOKIES

1 cup shortening	2⁄3 cup rice flour
1⁄2 cup granulated sugar	2⁄3 cup bean flour
1 cup brown sugar	1 tsp soda
1 tsp vanilla	3⁄4 tsp salt
2 well-beaten eggs	2 tsp Xanthan gum
	6 oz chocolate chips
	1 cup nuts

CREAM first 4 ingredients.

FOLD in eggs and beat entire mixture.

MIX dry ingredients.

ADD to shortening ingredients.

ADD nuts and chips.

DROP by spoonfuls 1⁄2" apart on cooking sheet.

BAKE at 300° for 15 minutes in greased pan.

May substitute 1 cup honey for the sugars.
                    Makes 100 cookies.

CHEWY CHOCOLATE COOKIES

1 1/4 cups shortening
2 cups sugar
2 eggs
2 tsp vanilla

1 cup bean flour
1 cup oat or rice flour
2 tsp Xanthan gum
3/4 cup cocoa
1 tsp baking soda
1/2 tsp salt
1 cup chopped nuts

CREAM shortening and sugar.

ADD eggs and vanilla. BLEND.

COMBINE flour, gum, cocoa, baking soda and
       salt.

BLEND into cream mixture.

STIR in nuts.

DROP by teaspoonfuls onto ungreased cookie
       sheet.

BAKE at 350° for 8-9 minutes. (Do not overbake!)

COOL for 1 minute.
                    Makes about 4 dozen

LEMON BARS

If you use butter, you can omit the sugar, but you need the sugar if you use margarine.

1 cup rice flour	1 cup butter
1 cup bean flour	½ cup powdered
2 tsp Xanthan gum	sugar

MIX thoroughly.

PAT down in 9" x13"" baking dish or pan.

BAKE 15-25 minutes at 350°.

FILL with canned or your own lemon pie filling.

WHEN cool, sprinkle with powdered sugar
                    or
FILL before baking and bake 25 minutes.

ALMOND OATMEAL COOKIES

4 cups quick-cooking oatmeal   2 beaten eggs
2 cups brown sugar   1 tsp salt
1 cup vegetable oil   1 tsp almond
       extract

MIX first 3 ingredients and let set overnight or for
     several hours.

MIX in rest of ingredients.

DROP from a teaspoon onto a greased baking
     sheet.

BAKE at 325° for 15 minutes.

REMOVE promptly when done.

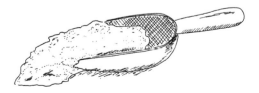

CHOCOLATE MARSHMALLOW COOKIES

1 cup puffed rice   1 cup coconut
1 cup chocolate chips   1⁄2 cup chopped walnuts
1 1⁄2 cup small marshmallows

COVER a small square baking dish with the rice.

POUR chocolate chips over the rice.

POUR marshmallows over the chips.

POUR coconut over the marshmallows.

POUR nuts over all.

BAKE 350° for 20 minutes.

PEANUT BUTTER SQUARES

1 (6 oz) pkg butterscotch or chocolate chips
1⁄2 cup peanut butter
3 cups puffed rice (or rice crispies)

MELT chips & peanut butter over hot (not boiling)
        water.

TAKE from heat and add cereal.

DROP on wax papered cookie sheet.

REFRIGERATE until firm.

BOUNTY BARS

1⁄2 cup shortening   1 cup coconut
3⁄4 cup honey   1 tsp almond extract
2 eggs slightly beaten   1⁄2 cup raisins
2 tbl milk (water)   1⁄2 cup walnuts
2 cups oatmeal
  (regular or quick)

CREAM shortening and honey together.

BEAT in eggs and milk.

STIR in remaining ingredients.

PAT mixture into a greased 9 x 13" pan.

BAKE at 350° for 15-20 minutes.

COCONUT MACAROONS

¼ cup rice flour   14 oz flake coconut
¼ cup bean flour   3 tbl Karo syrup
½ tsp salt   1 ½ tsp vanilla
⅔ cup milk (water)   ½ tsp almond extract

MIX dry ingredients.

MIX with remaining ingredients.

DROP from a spoon onto greased and floured
    sheet.

BAKE at 325° for 20 minutes.
                    4 dozen

CELEBRATION COOKIE

FORM a 8" circle with cookie dough (see sugar
    cookies).

BAKE in 400° oven for 10 minutes or until done.

COOL crust for 5 minutes.

LOOSEN edges of crust.

STIR together...
> 1 5 oz can vanilla pudding
> 1/3 cup peanut butter

GENTLY fold in 1/4 cup plain-yogurt

SPREAD over cookie crust.

SLICE a banana diagonally and brush with lemon juice.

LAYER on top of peanut butter mixture.

DRIZZLE warmed jam or jelly over cookie <u>before</u> serving.

SPRINKLE with dry roasted peanuts.

MEXICAN WEDDING CAKES

1 cup butter or margarine	7/8 cup rice flour
1⁄4 cup powdered sugar	7/8 cup bean flour
1/8 tsp salt	2 tsp Xanthan gum
2 tsp vanilla extract	1 cup chopped nuts
	powdered sugar

CREAM butter and sugar.

ADD salt, vanilla, flours, gum and nuts.

CHILL dough, covered, for a couple of hours or
overnight.

PREHEAT oven to 325°.

FORM dough into 1" balls.

PLACE on ungreased baking sheet.

BAKE 12-15 minutes.

REMOVE from oven and immediately roll in
powdered sugar.

COOL. May be frozen.
                    Makes 48 cookies

Note: Substituting 1 cup regular sugar totally

changes the texture of the cookie, making a very chewy and equally good cookie!

As a little boy, oldest son Harvey used to really love "spidercrotch".

OATMEAL SCOTCHIES (as in butterscotch)

3⁄4 cup unsifted rice flour
3⁄4 cup unsifted bean flour
1 tsp baking soda
2 tsp baking powder
2 tsp Xanthan gum
1 tsp salt
1 cup butter or margarine

1 1⁄2 cups packed
   brown sugar
2 eggs
1 tbl water
1 1⁄2 cups quick oats
   uncooked
1 12 oz pkg butter
   scotch morsels
1⁄2 tsp orange extract

PREHEAT oven to 375°.

COMBINE first 6 ingredients.

COMBINE butter, sugar, eggs and water.

BEAT until creamy.

GRADUALLY add flour mixture.

STIR in oats, butterscotch morsels and extract.

DROP by tablespoonfuls onto greased cookie
    sheets.

BAKE at 375° for 10-12 minutes.
            4 dozen cookies

BLUEBERRY OAT BARS

1 3⁄4 cups quick or regular oats	3⁄4 cup melted margarine
1 1⁄2 cups oat flour	2 cups fresh frozen blueberries
1 1⁄2 tsp Xanthan gum	
3⁄4 cup packed brown sugar	1⁄2 cup granulated sugar
1⁄2 cup chopped nuts	3 tbl water
1⁄2 tsp baking soda	2 tbl cornstarch
1⁄2 tsp salt (optional)	2 tsp lemon juice

COMBINE first 7 ingredients.

ADD margarine and mix until crumbly.

RESERVE 3⁄4 cup of mixture

PRESS remaining mix onto bottom of a greased
    11" X 7" glass baking dish.

BAKE 10 minutes.

COMBINE blueberries, granulated sugar and
2 tbl water.

BRING to boil; simmer 2 minutes, uncovered.

STIR occasionally.

COMBINE remaining 1 tbl water, cornstarch and
lemon juice.

STIR gradually into blueberry mixture.

COOK and stir about 30 seconds or until
thickened.

SPREAD over partially baked base to within 1/4"
of edge.

SPRINKLE with reserved oat mixture.

BAKE 18-20 minutes or until topping golden
brown.

COOL on wire rack; cut into bars.

STORE in tightly covered container.

PECAN PIE BARS

1 cup oat flour
1 tsp Xanthan gum
1⁄2 cup quick oats)
   (uncooked)
1⁄2 cup butter softened
3⁄4 cup packed brown
   sugar

3⁄4 cup corn syrup
1 cup chopped pecans
1 tbl oat flour
1⁄4 tsp salt
1 tsp vanilla
3 eggs

PREHEAT oven to 350°.

GREASE 9" square pan.

COMBINE first 5 ingredients.

PRESS into baking pan.

BAKE 15 minutes.

BEAT eggs, syrup, pecans, vanilla, salt and flour.

POUR over baked crust.

BAKE 25-30 minutes.

COOL on wire rack.

CUT into bars while still slightly warm.

One of my favorites...

MAPLE BARS

1 cup unsalted butter	2⁄3 cup rice flour
1 cup sugar	2⁄3 cup oat flour
or 2⁄3 cup honey	1 1⁄2 tsp Xanthan gum
2 tsp vanilla extract	4 tsp baking powder
2 tsp maple extract	2 cups rolled oats
2 large eggs	1 cup finely chopped walnuts
	1 cup flaked coconut

BEAT together butter, sugar, extracts, eggs.

SIFT flour and baking powder.

STIR into liquid mixture.

BLEND in oats, coconut, and walnuts.

SPREAD batter evenly in buttered 9" x13" baking pan.

BAKE for 50 minutes at 300°, until lightly browned.

COOL and cut into bars.

SCOTCH SHORTBREAD

1⁄2 lb butter
1⁄4 cup sugar
1 cup bean flour
2 cups rice flour
3 tsp Xanthan gum

CREAM butter and sugar

ADD flours and gum.

PRESS into 8" pan.

BAKE at 300° for 1 hour.

COOL and cut into squares.

RUSSIAN TEACAKES

1 cup butter or margarine
1 cup powdered sugar
1 tsp salt
1 tsp vanilla extract
2 cups rice flour
2 tsp Xanthan gum
1 cup finely chopped hazelnut or pecans
additional powdered sugar for rolling

PREHEAT OVEN TO 325°.

CREAM butter and sugar.

ADD salt and extract and mix well.

STIR in flour, gum and nuts.

DIVIDE dough into 1" balls and place 1½ inches
        apart on an ungreased cookie sheet.

BAKE 10 minutes.

ROLL in powdered sugar right away and allow to
        cool on rack.

WHEN cool, roll again. Rolling twice is important.

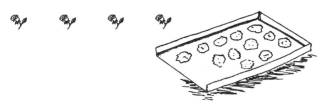

MAIN COURSES

"Fame is at best an unperforming cheat;
But 'tis substantial happiness to eat."

Alexander Pope

Come ye thankful people

Come raise the song of Harvest-home:

All is safely gathered in

Ere the winter storms begin.

...Henry Alford 1810-1871

CORN FLOUR (not to be confused with cornstarch) is great for pan frying. Corn meal works, but corn flour is crisper and very good.

CRISPY FRIED CHICKEN

1 cup corn flour	1 tbl water
2 tsp salt	2 3 lb. frying chickens,
1/2 tsp garlic salt	quartered
1/4 tsp pepper	shortening or cooking
1 egg slightly beaten	oil

COMBINE corn flour with next 3 ingredients in a
    sack.

SHAKE thoroughly.

COMBINE egg and water.

DIP chicken pieces in egg mixture.

SHAKE each piece of chicken in sack until coated.

PAN fry in large fry pan in hot oil about 1/2" deep,
    until golden brown on all sides.

REDUCE heat, cover, and cook about 40 minutes
    or until tender.

UNCOVER for the last 10 minutes for crisper
    chicken.
                        8 servings.

SWEET AND SOUR CHICKEN

2-3 lbs chicken, cut up   1 pkg onion soup mix
1 8 oz jar apricot preserves 1 8 oz jar Thousand
                                        Island Dressing

WASH chicken pieces and place in one layer in a
    baking dish.

SPOON apricot preserves on each piece of
    chicken.

SPRINKLE with onion soup mix.

POUR dressing over each piece.

COVER and bake at 350° for 1 ½ hours.
                    serves 4

ORANGE CHICKEN

1 6 oz can frozen orange juice   1 tsp oregano
1 juice can water   1/2 tsp ground nutmeg
1/4 cup dark brown sugar   1 medium onion-2/3cp

MIX all ingredients.

ADD to drained boiled, baked or fried chicken.

HEAT 30 minutes in frying pan or until warm.

BARBEQUED HAWAIIAN CHICKEN

1 cut up fryer
1/4 cup apricot preserves
1/4 cup Russian salad dressing
2 tbl dry onion soup mix

MICROWAVE chicken parts, covered, on Hi for 15
      minutes turning dish every 3 minutes.
GRILL over hot coals for 5 minutes.

COMBINE rest of ingredients and brush over
      chicken.
GRILL 10 minutes more or until done.

CHICKEN PIE

1 double crust portion of pastry
1 small boiled chicken cut up off the bone
2 egg yolks
1⁄2 cup sweet or sour cream (or chicken stock)

ROLL out 1⁄2 portion pastry dough and line a pie
    or baking dish.

FILL with chicken.

MIX and add eggs and cream.

COVER with rest of pastry.

BAKE at 325° for 1⁄2-1 hour until browned.

OPTIONAL: Add 1 cup peas or other vegetable
    chopped.

ROAST TURKEY

Make sure the bird is thoroughly rinsed inside and
out.
Thaw frozen turkeys to room temperature over
night before stuffing.
Allow 8 cups stuffing for a 10 pound turkey.

STUFF with Savory Stuffing (p. 120) or Cinnamon
Raisin Stuffing (p. 127)
TRUSS by tying legs close to the body and firmly
to the tail. Sew the stuffing cavity together
or fasten with skewers and lace with string.
PLACE breast side up, on a rack in an open
roasting pan.

RUB skin with butter or cooking oil.

PUT a piece of aluminum foil over the bird to cover
it loosely. (Do not let the foil touch the
heating element in an electric oven.)
ROAST at 325° until tender...

WEIGHT in pounds	HOURS
4 to 6	3-4
8 to 12	4-4 1/2
12 to 16	4 1/2-5
16 to 20	6-8
20 to 24	8-9

Half an hour before roasting time is up, turn back
the foil so the skin can brown.

Let stand for 20 minutes when done, to facilitate
carving.

AN EASIER WAY....

PREPARE turkey in the same way as above, but
use a roasting bag. Oven cooking bags
produce a very juicy product without the
cleanup and in a shorter period of time.
Follow directions on the box.

SAVORY STUFFING WITH OYSTERS
(for a 20 lb. turkey)

1 cup chopped celery	2 (or 3) jars raw oysters
1 cup chopped onion	2 tsp poultry seasoning
(optional)	or 1 tsp each basil,
½ cup butter or margarine	thyme, sage, and
1 bay leaf	celery seed
12 cups dry leftover bread	salt and pepper
cubes	2 beaten eggs

MIX together and stuff.

Or MICROWAVE in a covered dish for 4 minutes
on high. Let set 5 minutes.

THANKSGIVING VEGETABLES

2 pints brussel sprouts   ½ cup honey or maple
24 white pearl onions   syrup
20 oz preserved   2 tbl butter or margarine
   kumquats   2 tsp dried thyme
2-3 large semi-ripe pears ¼ tsp freshly ground
   peeled, cored, quartered pepper
½ cup apple cider   1 tbl chopped mint

CUT thin slice off bottom of each sprout, and cut
    an X in bottom.

PLACE sprouts in boiling water and blanche for
    5 minutes.

DRAIN & run under cold water, pat dry and set
    aside.

COOK onions in boiling water 7 minutes.

DRAIN & run under cold water, and pat dry.

SLICE roots off, leave whole and set aside.

DRAIN kumquats, rinse and reserve.

CUT pear quarters lengthwise into ¼" slices.

PREHEAT oven to 350°.

HEAT cider, honey, butter & thyme in small sauce
   pan until butter melts, stirring occasionally.

LAY vegetables in 4 rows crosswise in a 9"x 13"x
   2" ovenproof dish.

POUR cider mixture over vegies and sprinkle with
   black pepper.

COVER dish with aluminum foil and bake for
   45 minutes, basting twice.

UNCOVER and bake 15 minutes more until vegies
   are glazed and browned on top.

BASTE before serving.

SPRINKLE with mint.
                     serves 12

PERSIAN LAMB WITH PEACHES

1 lb of peaches or nectarines
                    or
a 1 lb can sliced peaches, drained
lemon juice
2 lbs lean boneless lamb shoulder
1 tsp ground cinnamon
1/2 tsp ground cloves
1/4 tsp pepper
2 tbl brown sugar
1 medium size onion, chopped
2 tbl lemon juice
4 tsp each cornstarch and water
salt
hot cooked rice
mint leaves
unflavored yogurt

PEEL and slice peaches.

SPRINKLE with lemon juice. (omit with canned
        peaches)

SET aside.

TRIM excess fat from lamb and cut into 3/4"
        cubes.

ARRANGE in a shallow 2 quart baking dish.

MIX together cinnamon, cloves, pepper and sugar.

SPRINKLE over lamb.

ADD onion and lemon juice.

COVER with a lid or plastic wrap.

MICROWAVE on Hi for 5 minutes and stir well.

MICROWAVE covered on Medium for 30 minutes
     stirring after 15 minutes or until meat is fork-
     tender.

LET stand for 5 minutes.

TRANSFER lamb to a plate and cover.

STIR together cornstarch and water.

STIR into lamb juices.

MICROWAVE uncovered on HI for 2-3 minutes,
     stirring every minute until bubbly and
     thickened.

STIR in the meat and spoon over the rice.

GARNISH with peaches and mint.

PASS the yogurt. (Omit if dairy products are a
   problem.)

May substitute pears for peaches.
               serves 4-6

❦   ❦   ❦   ❦

ROAST GOOSE

THAW goose.

REMOVE neck, giblets and loose fat.

SIMMER neck and giblets for gravy.

MIX and bake stuffing in a <u>separate</u> pan. (see
      stuffings)

PUT slice of onion and one or two celery stocks in
      cavity.

PLACE goose on rack in roasting pan.

COVER with tight fitting lid so that steam and
      juices remain.

(You may also like to try a roasting bag for a
speedier cooking time with very little mess. Follow
directions on box.)

BAKE in 400° oven using following chart.

WHEN done, remove cover for 10 minutes to
brown.

> 5-7 lbs - 1¾-2 hours
> 7-9 lbs - 2-2¼ hours
> 9-11 lbs - 2½-2¾ hours

Meat THERMOMETER will register 185°.

TO GO WITH THE GOOSE...

CORE red apples but do not peel.

CUT into ¼" thick slices.

FRY in butter until lightly browned.

DRAIN and sprinkle with sugar.

ROASTED WILD DUCK

½ cup chicken broth
1 6 oz can frozen orange juice concentrate
1 sliced orange

USE a prune-apple stuffing plus
> 1 tsp tarragon
> 1 tsp Rosemary
> 1 tsp parsley

MIX first 3 ingredients and put in roasting bag with
duck.

BAKE in a bag for 5-6 hours at 225°.

CINNAMON RAISIN STUFFING

5 tbl butter
large onion coarsely
   chopped
6 oz dried apple slices
1/2 tsp dried sage

3 cups day old wheat-
   free bread cut into 1"
   cubes (any sweet
   bread will do)
1 tsp cinnamon
1/3 cup raisins

HEAT butter in saucepan.

ADD onion and saute until tender (about
6 minutes).

STIR in apple slices, bread cubes and sage.

MIX well and stuff.

This is an old Oregon Recipe.

SALMI OF WILD DUCK

1 or 2 ducks, cut in quarters	2 small onions, thinly sliced
4 tbl butter	1 bay leaf
2 tbl bean or oat flour	2 cloves
1 cup red Bordeaux wine	1/2 tsp red pepper
2 cups stock or beef broth	sauce
salt and pepper to taste	1 pt small green olives
	chopped parsley

BROWN the duck pieces in butter until golden.

TRANSFER to a deep pot or casserole.

ADD flour to the pan and brown it in the butter.

STIR in the wine, stock and other ingredients except olives and parsley.

BRING to a boil and simmer for 5 minutes, stirring part of the time.

POUR the sauce over the duck pieces, cover the pot and simmer for 1 1/2 hours.

ADD olives and chopped parsley.

MEAT BALLS STROGANOFF

1 lb hamburger	1 tbl margarine
1⁄2 cup oatmeal or	1⁄2 lb sliced mushrooms
breadcrumbs	1⁄2 cup chopped onion
1⁄2 cup water	2 tbl rice flour
1 tsp salt	1 cup condensed beef bouillon
1⁄4 tsp pepper	1 tsp Worchestershire sauce
	1⁄4 tsp salt and pepper

1⁄4 cup non-dairy sour cream (Emo)

COMBINE first 5 ingredients, form into 1" balls and
brown in 3 tbl oil.

REMOVE from the pan.

SAUTE for 10 minutes in same pan, the
margarine, mushrooms and onion.
ADD flour and mix.

STIR in bouillon.

ADD meat balls, Worchestershire, salt & pepper.

COVER and simmer for 20 minutes.

ADD sour cream. (Emo)

SERVE over noodles. (See p. 27)

So easy and so good!

IMPOSSIBLE BACON QUICHE

12 slices bacon (½ lb) fried and crumbled
1 cup shredded Swiss cheese (4 oz)
⅓ cup finely chopped onion
2 cups milk or water
½ cup Biscuit mix (p. 3)
4 eggs
salt & pepper

HEAT oven to 350°.

GREASE 9"-10" pie pan.

SPRINKLE bacon, cheese and onion over bottom
of pan.

BLEND for 1 minute, milk, baking mix, eggs, salt &
pepper.

POUR into pie pan.

BAKE for 50-55 minutes until knife inserted in
center comes out clean.

LET stand for 5 minutes.

IMPOSSIBLE PIZZA PIE

2/3 cup chopped onion   1 1/2 cup milk (water)
1/3 cup grated Parmesan   3/4 cup Biscuit mix(p. 3)
3 eggs

HEAT oven to 425°. Grease 10" pie plate .

SPRINKLE onion and Parmesan in plate.

BEAT eggs, milk and Biscuit mix until smooth - 15
seconds in processor on high or 1 minute by hand.

POUR into plate.

BAKE 20 minutes.

SAUCE

1 can (6 oz) tomato paste   1/2 tsp garlic salt
1/4 cup water   1/2 tsp basil
1 tsp oregano   1/4 tsp pepper

SPREAD sauce over top.

LAYER remaining ingredients on sauce...

1/4 cup grated Parmesan
3 1/2 oz Pepperoni, sliced
1/3 cup chopped onion

1⁄2 cup chopped green pepper
1 cup shredded mozzarella

BAKE until cheese is light brown 15-20 minutes.

COOL 5 minutes.

                    6-8 servings

               ❀   ❀   ❀   ❀

My favorite...

IMPOSSIBLE HAM AND SWISS PIE

2 cups cut-up fully cooked ham
1 cup shredded natural Swiss cheese (4 oz)
1⁄3 cup chopped green or regular onions
1⁄4 tsp salt
1/8 tsp pepper   2 cups milk (water)
1 cup Biscuit mix (p. 3)   4 eggs

HEAT oven to 400°.

GREASE 10" pie plate.

SPRINKLE ham, cheese, and onions in plate.

BEAT remaining ingredients until smooth - 15
     seconds in processor on high or 1 minute
     by hand.

POUR into plate.

BAKE until golden brown and knife inserted in
    center comes out clean, 35-40 minutes.

COOL for 5 minutes.
        6 servings

❦   ❦   ❦   ❦

IMPOSSIBLE CHEESEBURGER PIE

1 lb ground beef	1/4 tsp pepper
1 1/2 cup chopped onion	1/2 tsp salt
1 1/2 cup milk (or water)	sliced tomatoes
3 eggs	1 cup grated cheddar
3/4 cup Biscuit mix (p. 3)	cheese

BROWN beef and onion, drain and spread in
    greased 10" pie plate.

BEAT next 5 ingredients for 15 seconds in
    processor on high or 1 minute by hand.

POUR over hamburger.

BAKE at 400° for 25 minutes.

TOP with 2 sliced tomatoes and grated cheese.

BAKE 5-8 minutes more until knife inserted in
center comes out clean.

POLISH LENTIL STEW

2 cups water   1 cup sliced celery
2 beef bouillon cubes or   1 cup chopped onions
   2 tsp broth granules   16 oz pureed tomatoes
1 cup dried lentils, rinsed 1 clove garlic, minced
8 oz Polish sausage sliced

BRING water and bouillon to boil in 4 qt Dutch
oven.

ADD all remaining ingredients in order given.

BOIL and stir for 1 minute.

REDUCE heat, cover, leaving cover ajar for 45-50
minutes.

If too thick, add water.
serves 4

CHEESE ENCHILADAS

12 corn tortillas   1 medium onion chopped
1 lb mild cheddar or   Red chili sauce (p. 173)
  longhorn grated   Chopped black olives

DIP tortillas one at a time in hot chili sauce for just
    a second to soften.

STACK on a plate ready to roll.

PLACE handful of cheese in middle of a tortilla.

ROLL up with end tucked under and place in
    baking dish.

RESERVE ½ cup grated cheese to top
    enchiladas.

COVER with red chili sauce.

SPRINKLE cheese on top.

BAKE in 400° oven for 20 minutes.

A family favorite, especially with homemade tortillas...

CHILI STACKS

1 lb hamburger
1⁄2 cup chopped onion
1 tsp salt
1 tbl chili powder
1⁄2 tsp oregano

1⁄4 tsp basil
1 15 oz can tomato
   sauce
5 corn tortillas
1 cup grated jack or
   cheddar cheese

BROWN hamburger & onion.

ADD salt, chili powder, oregano, basil & tomato
    sauce.

SIMMER 10 minutes.

LAYER tortillas, meat sauce & cheese (ending
    with sauce & cheese) in shallow baking
    dish.

BAKE at 350° for 15 minutes until cheese melts.
    10 wedges.

CHILES RELLENOS

PROCESS or blend 1 egg and 1/2 tsp baking
powder for each relleno for 60 seconds or
until batter is foamy.

POUR into 4"-5" circle in hot buttered skillet or
griddle.

PLACE cheese stuffed whole peeled green chili
(as in canned) on one half of batter & fold
over the other half as an omelet.

COOK for several minutes until golden brown on
both sides and cheese is melted.

SERVE immediately with green chili sauce.
(p. 174)

Dottie Force served this at a square dance. She said a salad and chips make this a good meal.

SKILLET TAMALE PIE

1 lb ground beef
1 tsp salt
1/2 tsp poultry seasoning
1 cup chopped onion
1 cup chopped green
   pepper
1 can undrained kernel
   corn

1 can stewed tomatoes
dash of lemon pepper
1 tbl chili powder
1 cup corn meal
1 cup sour cream
   (or non-dairy tofu)
1 cup grated Jack or
   cheddar cheese

MIX and cook first 3 ingredients. Drain.

ADD next 6 ingredients to ground beef and bring
      to a boil.

ADD chili, corn meal and sour cream and stir well.

COOK a few minutes to thicken.

SPRINKLE grated jack or cheddar cheese on top
      and let melt.
          serves 6-8

A very filling vegetable dish...

MEXICAN VEGETABLE CASSEROLE
(Spoonbread style)

1 1/2 cups fresh or frozen whole kernel corn
2/3 cup cornmeal
1/2 cup milk
1/2 cup chopped onion
2 slightly beaten eggs
1/2 cup chopped pepper
3/4 tsp salt
1/2 cup water
1/4 tsp pepper
1 cup chopped yellow summer squash or zucchini
several dashes pepper sauce
tomato & pepper slices
1 large tomato, chopped (1 cup)
1 cup shredded cheddar cheese (4 oz)

COMBINE corn, onion, green pepper, & water in
   medium saucepan.

BRING to a boil, reduce heat.

COVER and simmer for 5 minutes.

DO not drain.

COMBINE squash, tomato, 3/4 of the cheese,
   cornmeal, milk, eggs, salt, pepper, and
   pepper sauce.

ADD undrained vegetables.
MIX and turn into a a greased 1½ quart
     casserole.

MICROWAVE for 10 minutes on high, turning
     once,
                    or

BAKE uncovered in a 350° oven 45-50 minutes or
     till heated through.

TOP with remaining cheese, tomato and pepper
     slices.

MAKES 8 servings.

for an
ITALIAN VEGETABLE CASSEROLE

ADD ½ tsp oregano. (try basil!)

SUBSTITUTE 1 cup shredded mozzarella for
     cheddar.

I like these casseroles with the vegies finely
chopped.

Of course, if you have to stay away from all grains, this recipe is not for you!

ITALIAN RYE CRISP QUICHE

11 Rye Krisp crackers
  crushed reserving 1 tbl
3 tbl margarine, melted
1/4 cup zucchini,
  chopped
1/2 cup (2 oz) mozzarella
  cheese grated
3 eggs

1/4 plain yogurt
2 tbl tomato chopped
1/4 tsp Italian herb
  dressing
1/4 tsp salt
small can crab (opt.)

PREHEAT oven to 350°.

GREASE 8" pie plate.

COMBINE crackers, margarine, zucchini.

PRESS into bottom and sides of pie plate.

TOP with cheese.

BEAT eggs.

ADD yogurt, tomato, herb dressing and salt.

POUR over cheese.

SPRINKLE reserved tablespoon crumbs on top.

BAKE 30 minutes or until set.

LET stand 5 minutes.

If you do not have to avoid rye, try this...

RYE CRISP PIZZA

USE tomato paste to cover rye crisp which is
spread in a flat pan.

ADD crumbled cooked hamburger or sliced
sausage.

SPRINKLE with shredded mozzarella or jack
cheese.

MICROWAVE 2-3 minutes or broil until cheese
melts.

ZUCCHINI GARDEN STIR FRY

1 cup green pepper strips   1/2 cup cherry tomato
1 cup zucchini slices   halves
1/2 cup onion rings   3/4 cup (4 oz) crumbled
1/2 tsp oregano   feta
1 tbl cooking oil

COMBINE first 5 items in 1 1/2 quart bowl.

MICROWAVE on Hi for 4 minutes, stirring after 2.

ADD tomatoes and MICROWAVE 1 minute.

TOP with cheese

             OR

SAUTE first 5 items until tender but crisp (10
       minutes).

ADD tomato for 1 more minute.

ADD cheese.
       4 servings

Angelica Germana and I have known each other for 49 years!
She made this for our St. Ambrose Grammar School reunion.

ZUCCHINI ANGELICA

4 eggs slightly beaten	1⁄2 tsp salt
3 cups thinly sliced zucchini	1⁄2 tsp oregano
1 cup Biscuit mix (p. 3)	pepper & garlic
1⁄2 cup chopped onion	to taste
1⁄2 cup grated cheese	1⁄2 cup oil
2 tbl parsley	

COMBINE in greased oblong pan.

BAKE in 350° oven for 30-40 minutes or until
    brown.

For your stale breadcrumbs...

SPINACH-STUFFED PEPPERS

2 large green (or red or yellow) peppers
2 slices bacon diced
1 cup sliced fresh mushrooms
1 small carrot, shredded
1 can drained spinach
2 tbl wheat-free bread crumbs
1 tbl herb seasonings (p. 164)

CUT peppers lengthwise, remove seeds.

ARRANGE cut side down in microwavable dish.

COVER & MICROWAVE on high 2-3 minutes.

DRAIN & SET aside.

PLACE bacon in a 1 qt. casserole; cover with
        paper towels.

COOK on high 2-4 minutes until crisp.

REMOVE bacon, reserve drippings in casserole.

ADD mushrooms and carrot.

COVER.
COOK on high 3-4 minutes.

DRAIN.

STIR in spinach and bread crumbs.

FILL pepper halves with spinach mixture.

COOK uncovered on high 3-5 minutes (until
   heated)

TOP with bacon.

                    4 servings

HAM SUGGESTIONS

COMBINE
      strips of cooked ham
      1/2 cup brown sugar
      1 chopped onion
      1/2 cup ketchup

BAKE 425° until bubbly.

GRANDMA'S BALTIMORE CRAB CAKES

1 tsp dry mustard	1 lb crab meat (back fin)
1/2 tsp black & red	parsley
pepper mixed	1/2 cup any wheat-free
1 small egg	crumbs
1/3 cup (5 tbl) mayonnaise	

COMBINE ingredients.

LET set a day in refrigerator, then fry.

Grandma Potts - 10-89

CRAB IMPERIAL

GREASE ramikins (small oven-proof dishes)

PILE above crab cake mixture into ramikins.

DOT with mayonnaise and paprika.

BAKE 350° for 20-25 minutes.

Grandma Potts - 10-89

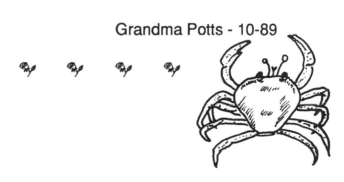

FRIED CLAMS

SHUCK and wash well in a colander under
    running water.

If clams have not had a cornmeal bath, open the
    stomachs with sharp knife and scrape out
    contents.

DRY between towels.

CUT away the black skin of the neck.

DIP clams in corn flour, then, egg beaten with little
    water, and lastly, wheat-free bread or
    cracker crumbs.

SAUTE until golden in a combination of
    3 parts vegetable oil
    2 parts butter

SERVE with tartar sauce or hot mustard sauce.

The cornmeal bath consists of soaking 1 quart of
clams and 1/4 cup cornmeal in 1 gallon of water.
Leave them soak for 3-12 hours.

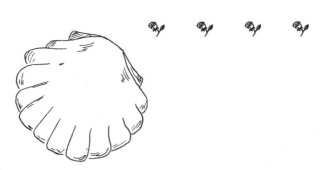

Brown rice has more fiber and good things for you than white rice.

PLAIN RICE

1 cup brown rice
2 1/2 cups water

PLACE in top of double boiler.

COOK slowly until liquid is absorbed - about 30-35
    minutes.

For white rice, use 2 cups water and cook
about 25 minutes.

SUBSTITUTE 1 can or 10 oz of beef or chicken
    broth for one of the required cups of water.

ORANGE RAISIN RICE

1 cup wild rice, cooked   ½ cup chopped parsley
3 cups long grain rice   ¼ cup grated orange
  (or 4 cups rice, cooked)   peel
¼ cup oil   1 tsp freshly ground
2 large onions, chopped   pepper
1 cup dark raisins   orange slices & parsley
½ cup chopped almonds   to garnish

HEAT onions in oil.

ADD to cooked rice.

STIR in rest of ingredients.
              serves 12

My favorite potluck contribution. Be prepared for requests for the recipe!

CURRIED RICE SALAD

1/4 cup Italian dressing   1/2 cup chopped onions
2 cups cooked rice   3/4 cup mayonnaise
1 10 oz pkg frozen peas   1/2 tsp curry powder
  cooked   1/4 tsp salt
1 cup diced celery

LET rice and dressing stand for 1 hour or more.

COMBINE rice, peas, celery, and onions.

COMBINE mayonnaise, curry and salt.

MIX together.

GARNISH with olives and green pepper.

May add 1 can tiny shrimp or water chestnuts or
    1/2 cup nuts.

RICE COMBINATIONS

To avoid hidden wheat or dairy contents, use
homemade soups. Otherwise, use 1 can of soup.

14 oz cream of mush-   14 oz cream of mush-
  room soup or white sauce   room soup or white
2 cups peas   sauce
7 oz can shrimp,   2 cups green beans
  crabmeat, or salmon   7 oz can small shrimp
2 cups cooked rice   2 cups cooked rice

14 oz tomato soup   14 oz tomato soup
1 tbl cornstarch   1 tbl cornstarch
2 cups succotash   2 cups peas
  (corn & limas)   1 can tuna
1 lb meatballs   2 cups cooked rice
2 cups cooked rice

14 oz tomato soup
1 tbl cornstarch
2 cups mixed vegies
sliced sausage
2 cups cooked rice

COMBINE one of these combinations in a skillet
        and cook on medium heat until thoroughly
        heated. (20 minutes)

❧   ❧   ❧   ❧

It won't be the same, but you can substitute tofu for the cheese if you must stay away from dairy foods.

BLUE CHEESE PASTA

4 cups water
2 cups wheat free pasta (p.   27)
3 cups frozen broccoli, carrots and cauliflower
2 tbl rice or bean flour
2 tbl butter or margarine
salt and pepper to taste
1 cup water
1/2 cup blue cheese (2 oz)
1/3 cup sour cream, yogurt or sour cream
    substitute

BOIL water in a large pot.

ADD 2 cups wheat-free pasta.

RETURN to boiling for 8-10 minutes or until almost
        tender.

ADD frozen vegetables to pasta and cook 5-7
        minutes more.

DRAIN. (Save 1 cup of the liquid.)

MIX flour and butter into the pot with salt and

pepper.
ADD the cup of liquid and stir until bubbly.

ADD pasta and vegies.

REMOVE from heat.

ADD blue cheese and sour cream or yogurt.

RETURN to heat through.

TOP with additional cheese.

SERVE at once.

OPTIONAL - add 1 or 2 cans clams, drained.

In spite of my purpose to keep recipes simple, husband Ed says you had better include this one anyway. It's more involved, but, it is excellent and it was <u>originally</u> made without wheat.

BLINTZES

6 eggs	2 cups water
1 tsp salt	oil for frying
1 cup potato starch	Filling

BLEND eggs and salt in blender or processor.

ADD potato starch and water.

BLEND until smooth, then pour into a pitcher.

HEAT a seasoned 6" iron or non-stick skillet until
    very hot.

GREASE well.

POUR in 3 tbl of batter, and swirl to cover pan.

POUR off any excess.

COOK on one side only until firm, about 1 minute.

TURN onto counter or board to cool.

REPEAT until all batter is used.

COVER each blintz with waxed paper and stack.

COVER with towel until filling is ready.

If you must avoid dairy products, you may want to
substitute tofu or use a fruit filling.

FILLING
1 lb farmers or ricotta cheese, 1 lb pot cheese or
well-drained cottage cheese, 1 tbl melted butter,

1 tsp granulated sugar, 2 eggs, 1⁄2 tsp salt
STIR all ingredients together until well-blended.

SPREAD blintzes on a counter.

SPOON a heaping tablespoon of filling into center
     of each blintz.

ROLL up each blintz and tuck in edges.

REFRIGERATE, covered, for a minimum of 2
        hours or a maximum of 2 days. If stacking,
        layer with waxed paper.

SAUTE in butter over low heat until golden brown
        on both sides.

SERVE with sour cream and/or fresh fruit.

POTATO LATKES (pancakes)

6 medium size potatoes   1⁄2 cup bean flour
1 onion   1 tsp salt
2 eggs   oil for frying

PEEL and grate potatoes into a mixing bowl.

SQUEEZE out liquid.

PEEL and grate onion into potatoes.

ADD eggs, flour, and salt and stir.

HEAT the oil in a heavy frying pan using enough
to cover the pancakes.

DROP the batter from a spoon into hot oil, making
pancakes 2-3 inches in diameter.

FRY over moderate heat until brown on one side,
then turn and brown.

LIFT out and drain on paper towel.
serves 4-6

SCALLOPED POTATOES (non-dairy)

SLICE potatoes thinly with a processor.

BARELY cover with water and bring to a boil.

COOK at medium heat until potatoes are soft and
have made their own sauce.

SEASON according to taste.

A very filling non-wheat meal...

SWISS POTATO PIE

2 lbs red or new potatoes   dash nutmeg
3 tbl butter   3 tbl balsamic vinegar
2 lbs Swiss chard   2 cups chicken stock
  (2 bunches) coarsely   pepper to taste
  chopped
1 shallot minced
2 cloves garlic minced

SLICE potatoes into very thin slices and set aside.

MELT 2 tbl butter in large skillet.

ADD chard, shallot and garlic.

WHEN chard has wilted, add vinegar and
    seasonings.

ALTERNATE layers of potatoes and chard in a
    large shallow buttered casserole dish.

POUR stock over layers so they are just covered.

DOT with butter.

BAKE at 375° for 50-60 minutes or MICROWAVE
    for 20 minutes at 50%.

SET stand 10 minutes and serve.
8 servings

CHICKEN STOCK

carcass of roasted turkey or chicken
(break up bones)
2 large onions, chopped (use processor)
3 carrots, peeled and chopped
1-2 leeks, thinly sliced both white & green
3 garlic cloves left whole
handful fresh parsley
2 bay leaves
1 tsp dried thyme
several black peppercorns
12 cups cold water

BRING to a boil in a large stock pot with cover.

LOWER heat to a gentle simmer for 3 hours partly
covered.
SKIM the froth.

STRAIN through sieve, pressing out solids.

LET cool and refrigerate or freeze.

Here's a milk-free cream of potato soup.

POTATO SOUP

4 cups chicken stock   1 tsp dried dill weed
2 cups diced potatoes   6 drops of hot pepper
1 grated carrot   sauce
1 tbl "herb mix" (p. 164)   1/4 cup parsley leaves

If you like onions, (and they like you!) add 2 cups
    of sauteed chopped onions.

COMBINE all ingredients except parsley in a
    stockpot.

BRING to a boil, then reduce the heat.

SIMMER for 25-30 minutes, until vegetables are
    soft.

TRANSFER 1 cup of vegetables and broth to a
    blender or processor.

PROCESS until smooth.

RETURN to the pot and add the parsley.

Optional - Add 1 tsp caraway seeds for a different
    flavor.

CREAMED VEGETABLE SOUP

Water or Stock	Chopped Vegies	Cornstarch or Flour	Milk	Amount
2 1/2 cups	2 cups	3 tbl	1 cup	4 cups
6 1/4 cups	3 cups	4 tbl	1 1/2	6 cups

COOK vegetables until tender then chop.

PUREE vegetables.

DISSOLVE cornstarch or flour in milk *.

ADD to puree.

BRING to boil.

ADD 1 tbl butter and season to taste with salt and pepper.

Optional - add onion powder, basil, coriander or whatever you feel good about!

* You may use soy milk, coconut milk, or non-dairy creamer.

TOMATO SOUP

2 tbl butter or margarine
1 medium onion, chopped
1 large carrot, chopped
4 cups regular-strength
   chicken broth

1 can (15 oz) tomato
   puree
3 tbl dry basil
¾ tsp sugar (optional)
½ tsp white pepper
Cheese croutons

MELT butter & add onion & carrot until both are
    tender. (30 min.)

STIR into the pan, broth, tomato puree, basil,
    sugar & pepper.

BRING to boil and simmer covered for about 15
    minutes.

SCOOP vegetables into a food processor or
    blender. Puree.

POUR vegetable mixtures back into pan.

HEAT.

LADLE into 4 bowls. Top with croutons.

BOUILLABAISSE

1⁄2 cup olive oil	1 lobster cut in small pieces
1 chopped carrot	1⁄2 lb. shrimp shelled and
2 chopped onions	cleaned or 1⁄2 lb crab meat
2 leeks cut small	1 dozen live mussels, clams
1 clove garlic	or oysters in shell
few grains saffron	

PUT first 5 ingredients in a big kettle.

COOK until brown.

PREPARE the shellfish and set aside.

ADD to kettle...

> 3 lbs of boned fish (a variety of fish is good)
> 2 large tomatoes or 1 cup canned tomatoes
>   cut up
> 1 bay leaf
> 2 quarts of boiling water or fish broth

SIMMER for 20 minutes.

ADD shellfish.

SIMMER until shells open (5 minutes).

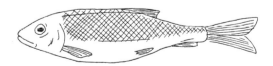

REMOVE top shell.
ADD salt and pepper to taste.

ADD the juice of 1 lemon.

ADD 1 cup white wine.

HERB SEASONING MIX

2 tbl dried dill weed
2 tbl dried parsley
1 tbl caraway seeds
1 tbl cumin seeds or 1 tsp ground cumin
1 tbl coriander seeds or 1 tsp ground coriander
1 tbl fennel seeds
1 tbl dried celery leaves or 1 tsp celery seeds

PROCESS all ingredients in a blender or
    processor.

STORE in a tightly capped jar.

Great for soups, stews and cooked vegies.
(Try a tablespoon in a pot of stew.)

A wonderful old favorite and so good for you...

TURKEY SALAD

4 cups chopped turkey
1 cup chopped apple
1 cup chopped walnuts
1 cup grapes
1 cup pineapple tidbits
1⁄2 cups mayonnaise or yogurt

COMBINE and serve on lettuce.

A filling, easy-to-fix dish.

CHICKEN AVOCADO

2 split avocados, pits   ¼ cup finely
   removed   chopped tomato
1 can chicken (7 oz)   Bacon Bits
few drops lemon juice   spicy-sweet French
                                            dressing

SCOOP out avocado, cut into chunks, and reserve
   shells.

SPRINKLE with lemon juice.

DRAIN chicken and break apart.

MIX gently the chicken, avocado and tomato.

SPOON into avocado shells.

TOP with salad dressing and bacon bits.

SAUCES

"More wives would learn to cook if they
weren't so busy trying to get meals."

Franklin P. Jones
Reader's Digest
March 1953

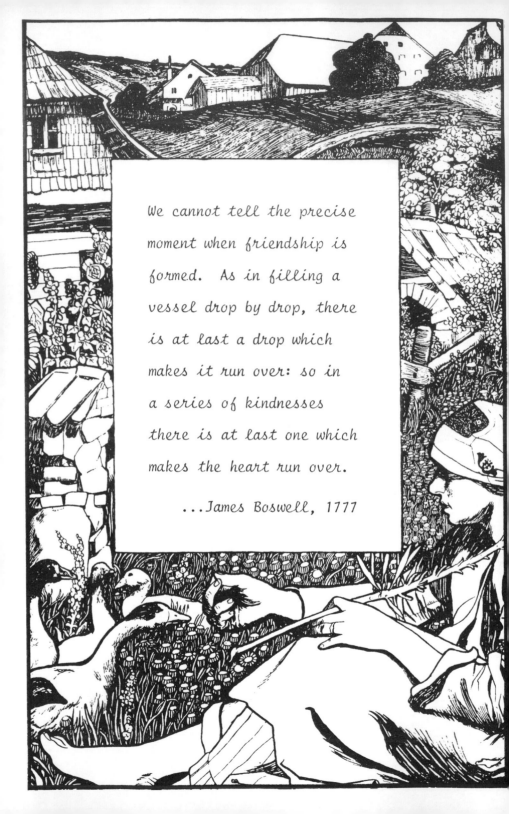

We cannot tell the precise
moment when friendship is
formed. As in filling a
vessel drop by drop, there
is at last a drop which
makes it run over: so in
a series of kindnesses
there is at last one which
makes the heart run over.

...James Boswell, 1777

You might assume a sauce would be wheat-free, but one look at the label would surprise you. If you make your own, you know what's in it. You also avoid problems with preservatives.

KETCHUP

1 12 oz can tomato paste	1 tsp oregano
1/2 cup lemon juice	1/8 tsp cumin
1/2 cup water	1/8 tsp nutmeg
1/2 tsp salt	1/2 tsp dry mustard
Dash garlic	1/8 tsp pepper

MIX and refrigerate.

1 3/4 cups

BARBEQUE SAUCE

1 cup Ketchup	1 tsp salt
1/3 cup worcestershire sauce	1 tsp brown sugar
1 tsp chili	1 cup water

HEAT until well mixed.

STORE in refrigerator.

BAR B QUE SAUCE PROVENCALE

1 8 oz can tomato sauce	2 tsp garlic powder
2 tbl frozen orange juice	1 ½ tsp tarragon,
concentrate	crushed
1 tbl water	¼ tsp pepper
	1 tbl onion powder

BRING all ingredients to a boil stirring
occasionally.

The tamari is wheat-free soy sauce, so this is safe...

TERIYAKI SAUCE

1 cup Mirin (Japanese sweet cooking wine)
1 cup tamari (can be found in health food
stores)
1-2 slices fresh ginger
1-2 cloves garlic minced

HEAT wine to boiling and cook for a few
minutes to remove the alcohol.

ADD tamari, ginger and garlic.

COOK for a few minutes longer.
makes 1 ½ cups

CUCUMBER SAUCE

(for fish, especially salmon)

1 cucumber peeled and sliced, lengthwise
1 cup yogurt or sour cream
1 tsp grated lemon rind
1/2 tsp lemon juice
dill, salt, pepper to taste

SLICE cucumber thinly.

SPRINKLE with salt.

SET aside for 15 minutes, then drain.

ADD rest of ingredients.
2 cups

Try this over pasta...

CLAM SAUCE

2 cans chopped clams   garlic
1 cup water   1 tbl parsley
2 tbl olive oil   salt

HEAT and serve.

ORANGE SAUCE FOR CHICKEN OR STIR FRY

2 tbl soy sauce	2 tsp cornstarch
(Tamari-wheat free)	2 tsp minced fresh
6 tbl water	ginger
2 tbl dry sherry	1/2 tsp red pepper
2 tbl orange marmalade	(optional)

COMBINE and heat thoroughly.
(Tamari can be found in health food stores.)

ORANGE SAUCE #2
(for rice or poultry)

1 can chicken bouillon
1 can orange juice concentrate(same size can)

HEAT and serve.

ORANGE SAUCE #3

1 cup sugar	1 cup orange juice
1/4 tsp salt	3/4 cup water
2 tbl cornstarch	1/4 cup lemon juice

BRING to a boil and let cool.

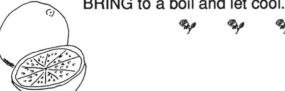

TACO SAUCE

1 can tomatoes or	1⁄4 tsp red pepper
1 1⁄2 cups	1 tsp salt
1 8 oz can tomato sauce	1⁄2 tsp celery salt
2 tsp chili powder	few drops tabasco
1⁄2 cup chopped onion	sauce

COOK for 10 minutes in saucepan.

RED CHILI SAUCE

1⁄3 cup shortening	1 tsp garlic powder or
1⁄2 cup bean flour	2 cloves minced garlic
2-3 tbl chili powder	1⁄2 tsp salt
2 cups tomato juice	Pinch cumin & oregano
2 cups water	

HEAT shortening and stir in flour and chili
    powder.

SAUTE until color starts to turn brown - this
    develops the flavor.

STIR in remaining ingredients until mixture
    thickens.

SIMMER 15-20 minutes.
Use with enchiladas.

GREEN CHILI SAUCE

3 cups chicken stock
1/2 cup chopped onion
1 large tomato chopped
(fresh or canned)
1 4 oz can diced green
peeled chilis

1/2 tsp garlic powder
1/2 tsp salt
1/8 tsp pepper
1/2 cup bean flour
1 cup water

COMBINE all but last 2 ingredients and bring
to a boil.

SIMMER for 15 minutes.

MAKE paste of flour and water and stir into
cooking sauce to thicken.

MEXICALI MEAT SAUCE

1 tbl olive or vegetable oil
1 tbl chili powder
1 tbl flour

3 cups water
1/2 onion, chopped
2 cloves garlic
1/2 tsp cumin

MIX first 3 ingredients into a paste.

ADD water and bring to a boil.

BOIL for 3 minutes.

ADD onion, garlic, and cumin.

USE with cooked beef or chicken for fajitas.

ADD sliced onions, peppers, etc.

Good in tacos, taco salad, enchiladas, etc.

HORSERADISH SAUCE

2 cups horseradish   2 tbl sugar
1/2 cup vinegar   1/2 pint sour cream

PEEL and grate the horseradish or put small
    chunks in the processor.

FOLD in commercial sour cream to the desired
    consistency. (May use non-dairy variety)

PACK in small sterile baby food jars.

PUT sugar on top to keep it from darkening.

REFRIGERATE.

HAM GLAZE

1 cup light or dark corn syrup	3 tbl prepared mustard
1/2 cup brown sugar, packed	1/2 tsp ground ginger

BRING all ingredients to a boil and boil for 5
  minutes.

BRUSH frequently on ham the last 30 minutes
  of baking.
          1 cup

Good on beef or green beans...

SOUR CREAM SAUCE

3 tbl butter	1 cup sour cream
2 tbl chopped chives	1 tsp dill weed

HEAT only enough to be able to pour over beef
  or green beans.

ORANGE TURKEY GLAZE

1 cup light corn syrup
1 cup orange juice
1⁄4 cup grated orange rind

MIX.
        2 1⁄4 cups

Great with poultry...

PLUM SAUCE

2⁄3 cup plum butter	1⁄4 tsp dry mustard
4 tsp orange juice	1⁄8 tsp Tamari *
2 tsp red-wine vinegar	(wheat-free soy
	sauce)
1⁄8 tsp grated orange	pinch of cardamom
rind	

COMBINE and cook over low heat stirring until
        mixture is smooth.

* found in health food stores

MAYONNAISE

(whole egg mayonnaise is softer than with only yolks)

1 whole egg or 3 egg yolks
1 tsp Dijon (or other style mustard)
1 tbl wine vinegar or lemon juice
1 cup vegetable oil
salt and pepper

PROCESS in a blender or processor, the egg,
      mustard, & vinegar for 3 seconds.

WITH processor still running, add oil a few
      drips at a time. (Put lip of measuring
      cup over the side of processing bowl
      and pour very slowly.)

MAYONNAISE will thicken.

TASTE and season with a few more drops of
      vinegar, salt and pepper if desired.
            makes 1 cup

WHEAT-FREE WHITE SAUCE MIX

2 cups nonfat dry
  powdered milk or
  non-dairy creamer
3/4 cup cornstarch
1/4 cup chicken bouillon
  powder

4 tsp onion powder
1 tsp dried thyme
1 tsp dried basil
1/2 tsp freshly
  ground pepper

Store in a tightly sealed container.

USE 1/4 cup of mix to 1 cup of water or milk.

STIR until smooth.

ADD 1 tbl butter.

HEAT and stir until thickened.

SEAFOOD SALAD DRESSING

8 sprigs watercress
6 spinach leaves (or chard)
5 sprigs parsley

PUT in bowl and cover with boiling water.

LET stand 5 minutes.

DRAIN and rinse twice in cold water.

ADD to processor with 1 cup mayonnaise.

ADD 2 tsp lemon juice.

PROCESS until blended.

SPREADS

We cannot tell the precise moment when
friendship is formed. As in filling a vessel drop
by drop, there is at last a drop which makes it
run over: so in a series of kindnesses there is
at last one which makes the heart run over.

James Boswell, 1777

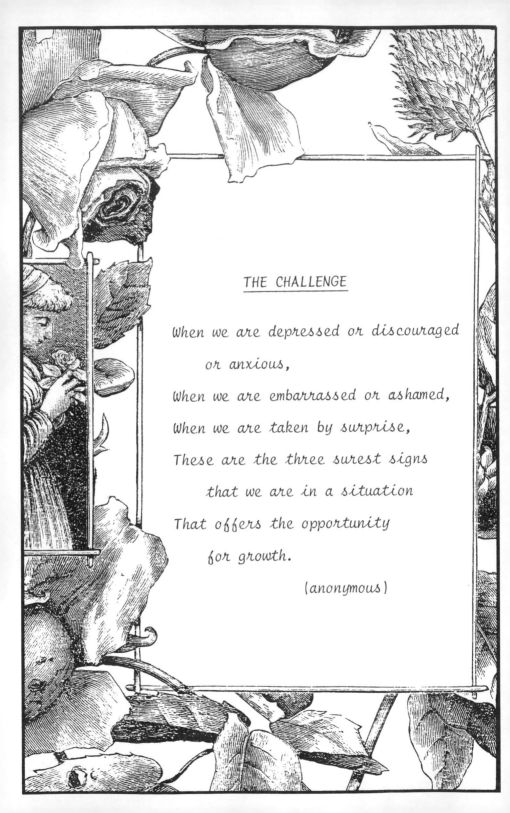

THE CHALLENGE

When we are depressed or discouraged
   or anxious,
When we are embarrassed or ashamed,
When we are taken by surprise,
These are the three surest signs
   that we are in a situation
That offers the opportunity
   for growth.

(anonymous)

NUT AND RAISIN SPREAD

1 medium orange
1 cup broken pecans
2 1⁄2 cups light raisins
3⁄4 cup mayonnaise or salad dressing
orange slices, celery sticks or crackers

QUARTER and seed orange, but do not peel.

PROCESS orange and nuts until finely
    chopped.

ADD 1⁄2 raisins and all mayonnaise.

PROCESS till raisins are chopped.

ADD remaining raisins and process till finely
    chopped.

PUT in covered container in refrigerator.

            May freeze up to 3 months.
            Thaw in refrigerator.

SPREAD on orange slices, celery or crackers.
            3 1⁄2 cups

SPINACH DIP

1 box (10-12 oz) frozen   1 tbl lemon juice
   chopped spinach   1/4 tsp salt
4 green onions   1/8 tsp ground
3/4 cup parsley sprigs   nutmeg
1 cup mayonnaise   dash cayenne
                                pepper

COOK and drain spinach.

COOL and set aside.

CUT onions in 1" lengths.

PROCESS onions in processor with parsley
    until finely chopped.

ADD mayonnaise, lemon juice, salt, nutmeg
    and pepper.

PROCESS until blended.

DRAIN spinach again and add to mixture.

PROCESS just enough to blend NOT puree.
    (2 on-off bursts)

COVER and chill.

                2 cups

Lots of good calcium here...

CLAM DIP

6 oz of cream cheese
1 tsp salt
1/2 tsp hot pepper sauce
1 tbl grated onion
1 71/2 oz can clam pieces (save juice)
1 cup sour cream

SOFTEN cheese at room temperature.

BLEND in next 3 ingredients.

ADD clams and 2 tsp clam juice to cream
       cheese.

STIR in sour cream.

CHILL at least 1/2 hour before serving.

GARNISH with sliced olives.

SERVE as dip for crackers, chips or raw
       vegetables.

2 cups

Another good source of calcium...

SALMON DIP

1 8 oz package cream cheese
1 tbl prepared mustard
1 tbl vinegar
2 tbl grated onion
1 tsp Worcestershire sauce
⅓ cup light cream
1 7¾ oz can salmon

SOFTEN cheese at room temperature.

BLEND cheese with the next 5 ingredients.

FLAKE the salmon and add to cream cheese.

BEAT until well-blended.

CHILL several hours to blend flavors.

SERVE as dip for crackers or chips.
                    2 cups

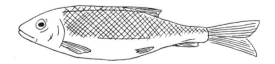

SHRIMP DIP

1 can small shrimp   several drops
1 large pkg cream cheese   pepper sauce
1-2 tbl grated onion   mayonnaise to thin
2-3 tbl parsley

MIX and chill.

May substitute non-dairy sour cream or tofu for cream cheese.

LIVER PATE

½ lb. liverwurst   2 tbl cream
3 oz pkg cream cheese   2 tsp Worcester-
2 tbl mayonnaise   shire sauce
                             1 tbl Sherry
                             1 tsp seasoned salt

MIX and chill.

May substitute non-dairy sour cream or tofu for cream cheese.

These little tidbits are so easy and so good!

HORS D'OEUVRES

1.   Little smoky links or the large ones cut
      in 1" lengths.

      HEAT in tomato sauce and serve in a
      chafing dish.

2.   Grind up dates, apples and nuts.

      ROLL in coconut and powdered sugar.

3.   Dates, cream cheese and honey.

      MIX cheese with a little honey and fill
      dates with mixture.

CEREALS

"Spare your breath to cool your porridge."

Rabelais

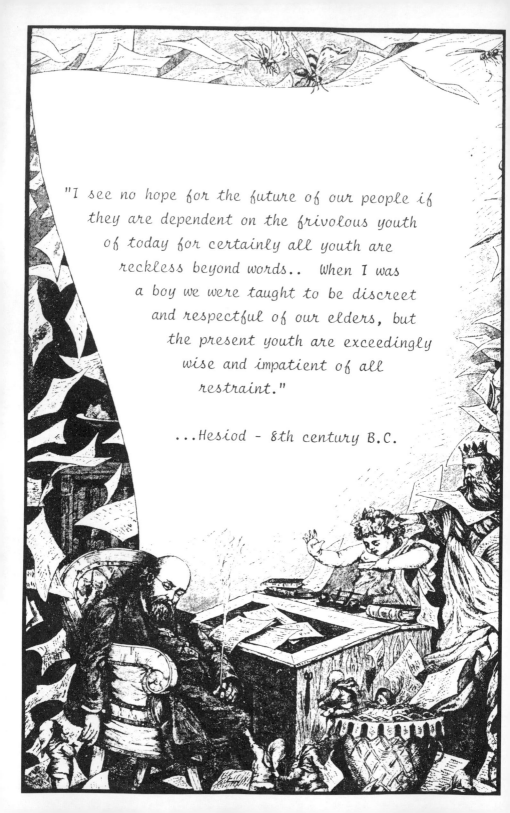

"I see no hope for the future of our people if they are dependent on the frivolous youth of today for certainly all youth are reckless beyond words.. When I was a boy we were taught to be discreet and respectful of our elders, but the present youth are exceedingly wise and impatient of all restraint."

...Hesiod - 8th century B.C.

It thrills me to death to know my friend, Linda, from Vanuatu (formerly New Hebrides) still uses my recipe for granola after 25 years!

GRANOLA

6 cups quick or old-fashioned oats - uncooked

HEAT in large roasting pan in 350° oven for 10
    minutes.

1/2 cup firmly packed brown sugar
3/4 cup oat bran
1/2 cup flaked or shredded coconut
1/2 cup raw or roasted sunflower seeds
1/3 cup sesame seeds
1 cup chopped nutmeats
1/2 cup vegetable oil
1/3 cup honey (increase to 1 cup if sugar is
    omitted)
1 1/2 tsp vanilla or almond extract

COMBINE oats and dry ingredients.

ADD oil, honey and extract.

MIX until dry ingredients are coated.

BAKE at 350° for 20-25 minutes stirring often
    to brown evenly.

COOL. Stir until crumbly.

STORE in tightly covered container.

❧   ❧   ❧   ❧

This looks great in a champagne glass!

STRAWBERRY BREAKFAST

LAYER sweetened berries with
　　　granola
　　　unflavored yogurt

❧   ❧   ❧   ❧

"As long as you're home, you'll eat a good breakfast!" my
Mother used to say. To speed up the porridge in the morn-
ing...

OATMEAL MIX

8 cups quick-cooking rolled oats	2½ tsp ground cinnamon
½ cup packed brown sugar	1½ tsp ground nutmeg
2 tsp salt	1½ cups raisins or dried fruit

COMBINE all ingredients in large bowl.

KEEP tightly sealed in 10 cup container.

USE within 6 months.

OATMEAL PORRIDGE

½ cup boiling water
½ cup oatmeal mix

ADD oatmeal to boiling water.

STIR and simmer over medium heat
        1-2 minutes.
                1 serving

SWEETS

"Oh, my friends, be warned by me,
That breakfast, dinner, lunch and tea
Are all the human frame requires..."

Hilaire Belloc

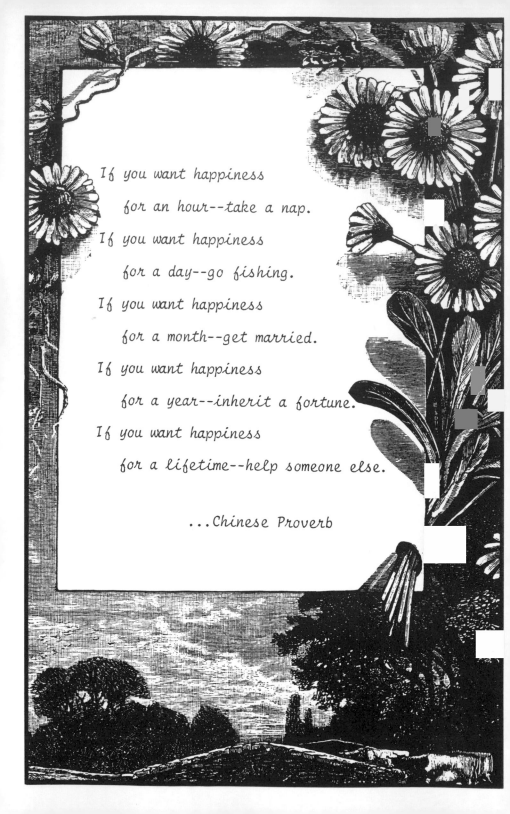

If you want happiness
   for an hour--take a nap.
If you want happiness
   for a day--go fishing.
If you want happiness
   for a month--get married.
If you want happiness
   for a year--inherit a fortune.
If you want happiness
   for a lifetime--help someone else.

   ...Chinese Proverb

A slip of paper was passed to me at a staff meeting...with this recipe from Paul Kyllo - a great taster of experimental recipes!

SWEET COCONUT RICE

2 cups cooked rice
1/2 cup coconut milk*
1/2 cup water

BRING water and coconut milk to boil in top of
a double boiler.

ADD rice, stirring only to keep rice from sticking
to pan.

PLACE top in the bottom of the double boiler.

COVER pot and simmer 12 minutes.

REMOVE from heat and let stand for
10 minutes.

DO NOT uncover until cooking time is up.
Tastes great warm, or cold with milk,
nuts, raisins etc.

*may use soy milk plus 1/4 cup flaked coconut

This is one good dessert, and a great way to use up leftover breads, even some of your not so special experiments!

STEAMED BREAD PUDDING

1 cup brown sugar   2 cups soy milk or water
1⁄2 cup raisins   1 tsp vanilla extract
2 cups buttered   1⁄2 tsp ground cinnamon
   bread   1⁄4 tsp salt
1⁄4 cup butter, softened
3 eggs

MIX sugar and raisins in the oiled top of your
       double boiler.
CUT buttered bread into 1⁄2" cubes.

PLACE the cubes on top of the sugar mixture.

BEAT eggs lightly in a medium bowl.

ADD remaining ingredients - don't overmix.

POUR egg mixture over bread cubes.

COOK over simmering water for about 1 hour
       and 30 minutes.

A knife should come out of the center fairly
clean.

STRAWBERRY NON-CAKE

SPOON a sauce of strawberries and a little
sugar over a canned pear half.

ADD nuts and "Cool Whip."
Tastes great!

*Making your own syrups protects you from
hidden wheat and preservatives.*

RASPBERRY SYRUP

1 pkg (10 oz) frozen raspberries
2 cups sugar
1/2 cup water

BRING all ingredients to boil.

SKIM off any foam.

POUR into hot sterilized jars and seal.
2 cups

You may substitute strawberries for raspberries.

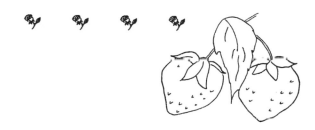

GRAPE SYRUP

1 cup grape juice
2 cups sugar
1 tbl lemon juice

COMBINE grape juice and sugar.

BRING to a boil.

SKIM off any foam.

ADD lemon juice.

POUR into hot sterilized jars and seal.
                2 cups

APPLE SYRUP

1 cup apple juice
2 cups sugar
cinnamon stick

BRING all ingredients to boil.

SKIM off any foam.

POUR into hot sterilized jars and seal.
                2 cups

ORANGE SYRUP

1 cup orange juice
2 cups sugar
2 tbl lemon juice

COMBINE orange juice and sugar.

BRING to boil.

SKIM off any foam.

ADD lemon juice and pour into hot sterilized
jars and seal.

2 cups

CHOCOLATE SYRUP

1/4 cup corn syrup   1 square bitter chocolate
1/2 cup sugar   1/2 tsp vanilla
1/2 cup water

COOK first 3 ingredients to soft ball stage.

REMOVE from heat and add chocolate and
vanilla.

THIN (if needed) by adding cream.

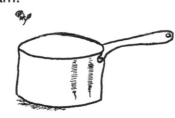

The only rationalization I can come up with for making candy, is that at least you know what goes into it - no hidden wheat or malt or preservatives. It makes a wonderful treat.

EASY MINTS

3 egg whites   Food coloring
6 cups confectioners sugar   mint extract

BEAT egg whites until stiff.

BLEND in sugar.

TINT and flavor.

ROLL out between waxed paper.

CUT patties.

LET dry overnight.

ROCKY ROAD CANDY

2 tbl butter or margarine
1 (12 oz) package semi-sweet chocolate
   morsels
2 cups nuts
1 (10½ oz) package mini-marshmallows

MELT morsels in glass bowl in microwave or
   over a double boiler.

STIR in rest of ingredients.

DROP from spoon onto waxed paper or

SPREAD in wax paper-lined 13"x 9"" pan.

CHILL until firm. (about 2 hours)

We used to sell this carmel corn every year at a 4H fundraiser at the Clackamas County Fairgrounds...

CARMEL CORN

Have 2 batches of popcorn ready...
2 cups brown sugar   1 tsp vanilla
1 cup margarine   1⁄2 tsp baking soda
1⁄2 cup corn syrup

MICROWAVE first 3 ingredients on Hi for 4
    minutes.

STIR after 2 minutes.
    (or boil for 5 minutes and bake mixture
    for 1 hour at 250° - stirring every 15
    minutes.)

ADD vanilla & baking soda.

MIX well.

ADD mixture to the popcorn.

FILL a brown bag with 1⁄2 of the popcorn
    mixture.

FOLD bag over and place in MICROWAVE for
    1 1⁄2 minutes.

TAKE bag out and SHAKE.

PUT bag back in MICROWAVE for another
1½ minutes.

SHAKE bag again.

SPREAD out to cool.

OPTIONAL - add pecans and almonds.

*When Bob Myers comes for Thanksgiving, he gets very
excited about these...*

PRALINES

2 cups granulated sugar   1 cup milk
1 cup packed brown   2 tsp Karo syrup
  sugar   4 cups pecan
1 cube (8 tbl) unsalted   halves or pieces
  butter

BRING first 5 ingredients to a boil in medium
saucepan.

COOK over low heat for 20 minutes.

STIR in pecans and cook until mixture forms a
soft ball when dropped into cold water.

STIR well and drop by spoonfuls onto waxed
　　paper.

COOL and wrap individually with waxed paper.
　　2½ dozen

NUT CLUSTERS

½ lb. Spanish peanuts (or almonds)
7-8 oz semi-sweet chocolate chips (2 cups)

MELT chocolate in double boiler.

REMOVE from heat.

ADD nuts and stir.

DROP onto waxed paper.

CHILL for 12 hours.

May substitute dry cereal for nuts.

SKILLET TOFFEE

3 cups sugar   1 cup chocolate chips
1 lb butter   1/2 cup chopped walnuts

COOK until candy thermometer registers 310°.

POUR into greased pan.

ADD chocolate chips on top.

SPREAD with a knife as they melt.

CAROL'S FUDGE

1 pkg chocolate chips	1 small can
1 tsp vanilla	evaporated milk
3⁄4 cube butter	10 marshmallows
2 cups sugar	(7 oz)

COMBINE chips, vanilla and butter into a bowl.

PUT sugar, milk and marshmallows into a pan.

WHEN sugar mixture comes to a rolling boil,
cook for 5 minutes only, using a wooden
spoon to stir.

POUR over chocolate chip mixture.

ADD nuts, (optional) beat and put into buttered
dish.
OR

MICROWAVE butter in 4 qt bowl on high for
1 minute or until melted.

ADD sugar and milk and MICROWAVE for
5 minutes or until mix comes to a rolling
boil.

STIR after 3 minutes. MIX well.

MICROWAVE for 5 1⁄2 minutes more, stirring
    after 3 minutes.

STIR in chocolate pieces and remaining
    ingredients.

BLEND well.

POUR into greased 13" x 9" pans.

COOL before cutting.
          3 lbs.

May substitute 1 cup peanut butter for
chocolate chips.

As close as you can come to wheat and dairy-free ice cream.

PEAR SORBET WITH PEAR BRANDY

2 lbs fresh ripe pears (Bartletts are excellent!)
1 tsp fresh lemon or lime juice
2 tbl pear brandy

PEEL, core and stem the pears.

PUREE the pears with the lemon juice.

TRANSFER to an ice cream freezer.

CHURN until a slushy consistency is achieved.

ADD pear brandy and churn to combine.

TASTE!

PLACE in container just large enough to hold
     the sorbet and COVER tightly.

FREEZE for several hours.

LET soften slightly before serving.

Matt Kramer's column in the Northwest Magazine section of THE OREGONIAN, 1989.

BEVERAGES

"That which the fountain sends forth returns
again to the fountain."

Henry Wadsworth Longfellow

The finest gift
we can give
to our age and
time is the gift
of a constructive
and creative
life.

unknown

ENERGY FLIP

½ banana   1 cup buttermilk
1 scoop sherbet   1 tbl protein powder

BLEND.

The buttermilk and sherbet combination are
what makes the drink!

ORANGE BLUSH

1 cup fresh strawberries
4 cups orange juice
3 ice cubes

MIX berries, orange juice and ice cubes to
        gether in blender until smooth.

serves 2

ORANGE PICK UP

1 egg
1 cup orange juice
Honey to taste

BLEND until smooth.

serves 1

PINK SUNRISE

1 cup fresh strawberries
3 cups pink grapefruit juice
1 banana

MIX together in blender until smooth.

serves 2

SUPER FRUIT SHAKE

6 large ripe strawberries	1 tsp honey
1 large banana	3 ice cubes
1 5½ oz can apricot or peach nectar	

BLEND.

INDEX

E

F

Q

R

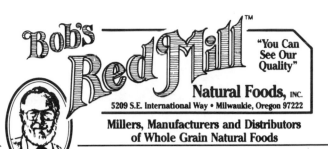

Natural Foods, INC.

5209 S.E. International Way • Milwaukie, Oregon 97222

Millers, Manufacturers and Distributors
of Whole Grain Natural Foods

WHEAT FREE
WHOLE GRAIN
PRODUCTS

All of the natural whole grain, wheat-free products listed in this book are sold under the Bob's Red Mill brand label and are available at finer stores throughout the U.S.A. Call or write for a Bob's Red Mill Mail Order Catalog or for the name and address of a store near you.

Bob's Red Mill Natural Foods
5209 S.E. International Way
Milwaukie, OR 97222
(503) 654-3215 • Fax (503) 653-1339

TO YOUR GOOD HEALTH

Bob Moore